furniture care:

REPAIRING & RESTORING chairs

furniture care:

REPAIRING & RESTORING chairs

professional techniques to bring your furniture back to life

WILLIAM COOK
W. J. COOK & SONS
PHOTOGRAPHY BY JOHN FREEMAN

LORENZ BOOKS

This edition is published by Lorenz Books
an imprint of Anness Publishing Ltd
Blaby Road, Wigston
Leicestershire LE18 4SE
info@anness.com

www.lorenzbooks.com; www.annesspublishing.com

If you like the images in this book and would like to investigate using them
for publishing, promotions or advertising, please visit our website
www.practicalpictures.com for more information.

A CIP catalogue record for this book is available from the British Library.

Publisher: Joanna Lorenz
Project Editors: Charlotte Berman, Lucy Doncaster and Claire Folkard
Text Editor: Alison Bolus
Designer: Lisa Tai
Photographer: John Freeman
Technical Director: Paul Lyon, W. J. Cook & Sons
Production Controller: Pirong Wang

Previously published as part of a larger volume,
The Complete Guide to Repairing and Restoring Furniture

PUBLISHER'S NOTE
Although the advice and information in this book are believed to be accurate and
true at the time of going to press, neither the authors nor the publisher can accept
any legal responsibility or liability for any errors or omissions that may have been
made nor for any inaccuracies nor for any loss, harm or injury that comes about
from following instructions or advice in this book. Before you begin any
restoration task, you should know how to use all your tools and equipment
safely, and be sure and confident about what you are doing.

CONTENTS

INTRODUCING CHAIR RESTORATION

Whatever the date, period or style, every chair eventually needs repair or restoration by the very nature of its construction. The continuous movement of the mortise and tenon joint combined with the gradual perishing of the original animal glues always makes chairs work themselves loose. In the past, repairs were often simply fashioned to make the chair usable, sometimes not even in the timber of the original – today it is a different story.

Before the burgeoning interest in antiques (not to mention their rapidly increasing value), chairs were considered as little more than secondhand pieces of furniture. It was not uncommon for chairs that had become loose to be strengthened by elaborate blacksmiths' brackets, which, ironically, took more time to make than simply knocking apart the chair and undertaking the repair correctly. But with the passing of time two major changes have taken place: the chair has assumed its own character and it has become steadily more valuable.

Understanding the construction of the piece, including the cabinet-making techniques used during its period, is vital when restoring chairs. Approached incorrectly, the easiest of tasks can soon develop into a major undertaking. Just as important as employing the relevant restoration method is access to the correct tools, a suitable work environment and, when necessary, antique timbers to patch damaged areas. Before beginning any restoration project, it should be thought through, and possible problems should be analysed and the best solutions realized. It makes no sense to begin gluing a chair together and then discovering that a cramping jig or an extra pair of hands is needed. Equally, if a set of chairs must be knocked apart and all the components have not been individually labelled, many hours can be spent trying to piece the individual chairs back together. Also important is the understanding of how and why a design developed and changed. Increasingly, research is needed to work out what was originally present but has subsequently been lost or changed – for instance, mouldings or mounts may have been altered or replaced to suit the contemporary fashion. The aesthetics of a chair can be rebalanced just by the removal of a later addition, and the correct replacement, or by the chair being returned to its correct height or proportion. The same applies to the upholstery, with different periods, styles and countries each employing their own methods and types.

A huge responsibility rests upon the shoulders of the antique chair restorer. In front of him is a piece of history, often with a surface that has developed its unique qualities over centuries. This uniqueness can be lost in an instant if the restorer applies the wrong methods. It is this skill of knowing how and what to do – and in many cases what not to do – that is the difference between a competent restorer and an amateur. So if in doubt, always consult an experienced restorer. If considerately approached he is usually willing to offer advice and say if he thinks a project is too adventurous.

Those who can handle the tools of antique restoration correctly should consider further education. There are a number of college courses designed to train the student restorer. Some would say that before attendance the student should already be trained and even qualified as a competent cabinet-maker, the restoration course simply acting as another step. Unfortunately, in today's hectic lifestyle, it is not always possible to gain previous cabinet-making experience. Restoration courses can range from a few months to

Left: An early 18th-century double chair-back settee with superb colour and patination that must be kept at all costs.

Above: *What may first appear as minor damage will often turn out to involve major structural repair.*

Above: *A selection of smith-made brackets, which were used to act as temporary strengtheners on loose chairs.*

one, two or three years. It should be remembered that after the completion of any course the gulf between classroom and workshop practice is wide. Nothing will replace the hours spent at the bench, honing and developing one's skills and working with experienced restorers who have spent a lifetime learning their craft.

Another development to be aware of is the debate of restoration versus conservation. There now exist two schools of thought: one advocates that a piece should be restored and, with the use

Below and right: *When upholstering, it is important not to spoil the aesthetic line of a chair and to allow its elegant form to be seen.*

of old or breaker pieces of timber, returned to a state in which the work is, as far as possible, unnoticeable; the other advocates that repairs should be carried out sympathetically but without blurring the line between old and new. While both sides have merit, from a commercial perspective, restoration wins the argument. Some techniques simply involve regluing loose joints and broken legs or attending to worn runners or lost stops, but the debate begins when a leg or a piece of veneer is lost. As illustrated in this book, a requirement of any serious workshop is an adequate breaker store. This will consist of timbers dating from the 17th, 18th and 19th centuries, hopefully to match the colour, grain and texture of a chair under repair. The conservator will argue that any new components should be manufactured from new timber and simply matched in as well as possible. This argument, while having some validity in rare pre-16th-century chairs when interest is largely scholarly, carries little weight with later furniture. In 17th, 18th and 19th-century chairs, a seamless repair is far more desirable. But both restorers and conservators would agree that any colour and patination the chair has developed should be left unaltered.

This understanding of colour and surface is vital because while previously the restorer would pass the chair to the

polisher to perform any necessary colouring, polishing or waxing, it is now common to find a restorer acting as both cabinet-maker and polisher. This dual role means that the restorer has to have a large area of expertise and not only be able to colour in small repairs but also, when required, polish entire sets of chairs. The importance of the restorer is increasing greatly as both the trade and public are buying more antique chairs that require attention before they can be sold or used. The next generation inheriting chairs is realizing the value of their legacies and appreciating the skill and workmanship involved in the original construction. Owners know that their chairs must be well cared for and restored if they are to survive and be appreciated by future generations.

Those who are prepared to invest time in learning their craft thoroughly while building up their historical knowledge, not to mention their supplies of timber, and increasing their practical ability, can be assured of a rewarding and satisfying interest or career. It should be remembered though that, as with everything in life, what one puts in is what one takes out – and never more so than in the field of antique chair restoration.

HISTORY OF CHAIRS

One of the most imposing symbols of authority throughout history has been the chair. It was the throne upon which the monarch sat when dispensing justice, and the term "chairperson" still refers to a person in a position of authority. While the material, style and design of the chair have all changed, its basic construction has remained constant, and, whatever its origin, the finest examples are still highly sought after by collectors all over the world.

The chair was one of the scarcest items of furniture to be found in the large halls of medieval Europe. Its use would have been reserved for the master, with the rest of the household sitting on stools or benches. Indeed, the 1594 inventory of Gilling Castle, Yorkshire, England, notes that the great chamber contained 28 stools but only one chair.

There were several styles of chair during the Middle Ages and latter part of the 15th century. Box chairs probably developed from early coffers, which had had the back and front posts continued to form supports for the back and arms. Indeed there are examples dating from the late 15th and early 16th centuries in which the seat lifts to give a storage area below, like a coffer. Such examples, known as close chairs, were often elaborately carved to emphasize the importance of the user, and, for added comfort, were supplied with a down cushion covered in the finest velvet material.

The next step was the development, or rather removal, of the boxed section below the sitter, with bold turned legs, joined by low stretchers, replacing the uprights. As with the majority of furniture of this period, the construction was of oak.

During the first part of the 16th century, a second important style of chair emerged and became popular throughout Europe. This was the Italian X-frame chair, which was descended from the ancient Roman high-status curule chair – an upholstered folding seat with curved legs. The X-frame chair consisted simply of webbing strung between side frames to form a seat. The side frames were often covered with expensive velvet or gold cloth, and a cushion was placed on the webs for greater comfort. It is unusual for these chairs to survive, because they

Left: *A 17th-century oak box-seat armchair showing how storage was combined with seating from the 15th century to the 17th century.*

were often made of beech, which is prone to infestation. Their development is important, however, as they were the first properly "upholstered" chairs.

A third type of early chair was the back stool. In its simplest form, and as its name suggests, this was a stool with an added back. Its chief characteristic was that its back legs descended vertically from the seat level to the floor. Interestingly, it was called a back stool because all chairs before the late 16th century had arms.

A final category of chair, less elaborate and much easier to make, was the thrown chair, which was usually made from ash, elm or yew. It was constructed of interlacing struts and rails, heavily turned (or "thrown" as it used to be called) with knob and ring decoration. Rather than the mortise and tenon joints found on the X-frame or box chair, the joints would consist of tapering dowel joints. Country craftsmen produced thrown chairs following designs that were handed down from generation to generation, and early examples may be seen in illuminated manuscripts from the 13th and 14th centuries. It is from these earliest designs that, during the 17th and 18th centuries, many regional variations of chair evolved throughout Europe and America. Perhaps the most famous of these rural

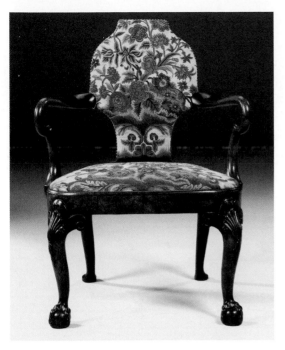

Left: *A prime example of how during the late 17th century decorative walnut was used both in the solid and veneer and covered with fine needlework.*

introduction of a new and distinctive type of walnut chair. It had a wide, shaped back, centred by a veneered or carved vase-shaped splat, above a curved seat, and would stand on cabriole legs often finished with pad feet. The earliest examples were strengthened with stretchers, but these were later abandoned in favour of a cleaner line. Later ball and claw or lion's paw feet were favoured in place of pad feet. It was from this point that the true diversity of style and function can be seen. Armchairs covered in needlework or velvet were designed to sit beside open fires, salon chairs were destined for the drawing room and shaped veneered back chairs, with their drop-in seats, were designed to be used at the dining table.

The Palladian movement of the early to mid-18th century, which reflected a revival of interest in classic Roman styles, coincided with the increased use of Cuban mahogany in furniture making in response to a French embargo on the export of walnut. Mahogany, with its dense grain, was ideally suited to the rich carving demanded by this architecturally inspired movement, and there developed a new type of chair, the Gainsborough, to adorn the galleries, libraries and drawing

chairs is the Windsor, with its solid wooden seat, turned legs and stick back. The design of thrown chairs has remained remarkably consistent since the 18th century, although features such as cabriole legs, pad feet and pierced back splats have been incorporated from time to time. They were then, and have remained, the chairs of the masses.

The box chair, however, underwent numerous changes, often taking more than one direction in its evolution. The French caquetoire, or gossip chair, became fashionable toward the middle of the 16th century. It had a seat that narrowed toward the tall, narrow back and splayed arms. By the end of the century, a simple chair known as the farthingale evolved. Named after the whalebone-hooped petticoats that supported the large skirts then fashionable, the farthingale chair allowed a lady to sit without becoming wedged between the arms (it had none).

During the mid-17th century, armchairs would often have had elaborate carved uprights, stretchers and backs, the

backs being combined with cane, velvet or leather. Oak remained a popular wood, but walnut – which was cheaper and could be more easily turned and carved – was becoming increasingly popular.

Comfort was also playing an increasingly important role in chair design: the angle of the back became less upright, and fully upholstered backs and seats were introduced. The walnut show wood was, on occasion, being replaced on the finest chairs with gesso, which was then carved, painted and gilded. While during the 15th and early 16th centuries chairs had been produced by coffer-makers, by the late 17th century a new breed of cabinet-maker, including Thomas Roberts and Daniel Marot, became closely associated with designing chairs. Marot was largely responsible for promoting the new Anglo-Dutch style. The early part of the 18th century saw the

Right: *By the mid-18th century, the finest mahogany Gainsboroughs were festooned with foliate carving.*

rooms of elegant country houses. Later in the century, with the emergence of designers and furniture-makers such as Thomas Chippendale (1718–79), William Ince (d.1804) and John Mayhew (fl.1758–1804), combined with the need to illustrate one's wealth, wonderfully carved sets of dining chairs, heavily influenced by the rococo and French style, began to emerge.

The next significant change in fashion was the emergence of neoclassical designs and influences during the second half of the 18th century. The architect and furniture designer Robert Adam (1728–92) oversaw the introduction of a lighter, more classical look, and the use of gilt decoration with delicate carved foliate and Greek mythology themes began to prevail. The requirement for a finer, more elegant impression toward the end of the 18th century, as championed by Thomas Sheraton (1751–1806), led to chairs also being decorated with japanning, paint and gilt.

During the early 19th century, the trend toward a finer line of construction began to be reversed, with chair designs being more affected by the growing

interest in other cultures and histories. In Europe, Greco-Roman and Egyptian themes were rapidly adopted, while in France these same ancient cultures provided the inspiration for the Empire furniture encouraged by Napoleon, himself an emperor.

Designs were varied and, during the 18th and 19th centuries, a number of new types of chair emerged. These included the bergère, a chair with a mahogany or rosewood frame supporting a canework back and seat panels, the hall chair, with its solid mahogany back and seat, and the reading chair, with its unusual design allowing it to be sat on in reverse and, on the finest examples, an arrangement of trays, candle slides and reading slopes.

With the emergence of the merchant classes during the mid- to late 19th century, chair production was vastly increased. Mahogany, now cheaper to import, was more commonly used. With the emphasis on function rather than fashion, chairs become bolder and more robust in design. Outside the main stream of commercial development, however, completely different thoughts

about furniture were being expressed. William Morris (1834–96) was one of those in the Arts and Crafts movement who championed traditional handcrafting methods over the poor quality of much machine production. In France, the natural, curving forms of the Art Nouveau movement, led by such makers as Emile Gallé, gave a completely new look to chairs.

In the 20th century, a fresh approach to design emerged, with the Art Deco movement using old and new techniques of furniture decoration – from lacquering to covering in mirror glass – to produce pieces that looked thoroughly modern. Later in the century, new materials, including chrome and laminates, were experimented with, producing landmark pieces such as the American designer Charles Eames's classic rosewood laminated chair of the mid-20th century. With the rapid increase in communication networks compared to the 18th and 19th centuries, designs went in and out of fashion much more rapidly than in previous historical periods and reached a more global audience.

Above: *A mid-20th-century, laminated birch dining chair designed by Charles and Ray Eames.*

CHAIR CONSTRUCTION

All antique chairs were individually made and so subject to minor variations. These variations can be accounted for not only by the chair's date of origin but also by its place of manufacture; they can even point to a particular cabinet-maker. For this reason, prior to any restoration, a close inspection should be made of a chair's construction so that any repairs can be carried out in as close a style as possible to the original cabinet-maker's work.

Unlike modern chairs, an antique chair can incorporate numerous construction methods. As a general rule, the earlier the chair the simpler the construction will be. For instance, the thrown chair dating from the medieval period has simple tapering dowel joints holding the legs and arms to the seat. At the same period, an early settle or framed chair will incorporate mortise and tenon joints. For extra strength, these will have a dowel drilled through and fitted into the tenon. By the late 17th century, most quality chairs have a mortise and tenon jointing the legs to the frame. During the 19th century, dowel peg joints often replaced the traditional mortise and tenon.

Corner blocks also altered over the centuries. These blocks, known as webs, were cut into rebates in the seat frame in the 18th century. However, on a chair with a drop-in seat, they can simply be small solid corner blocks that help to secure the corners of the seat rail and act as supports for the seat. By the mid- to late 19th century, the blocks were larger, solid triangles and were screwed to the inside of the frame.

Stretchers are another construction detail to look for. Again, like all the other features, the date of manufacture of the chair often dictated their form. Their use declined generally by the 19th century.

Varying designs of backs have been used, ranging from plain stick backs on perhaps a thrown chair or Windsor to the most fabulous carved interlace backs on the finest of Chippendale's chairs. If the seat was a stuff-over example, then a "shoe", which is basically a shaped cover piece, would have been placed over the upholstery. The shoe was designed to hide the holding tacks at the back of the seat frame.

Right: *The illustration shows the basic components of a chair with a classic drop-in seat.*

upright

drop-in seat

cabriole leg

tenon

top rail

back splat

corner block

seat rail

mortise

corner block

ear piece (bracket)

Right: *With a stuff-over seat, certain constructional changes are made in the manufacture of the chair.*

stuff-over seat

turned leg

back rail

upright

back splat

corner web

seat rail

mortise

tenon

Tools, equipment and materials

The right tools, equipment and materials are the lifeblood of any restorer. Often passed from generation to generation, they must be cared for and used with the skill they deserve, for without them even the most gifted of restorers will be unable to undertake the most basic of restoration jobs.

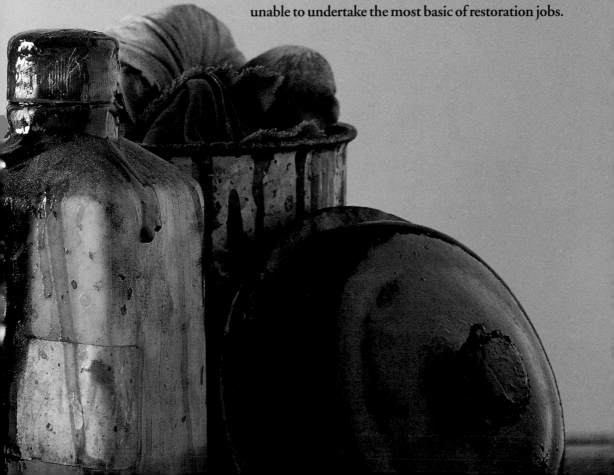

CREATING A WORKSPACE

More often than not, financial limitations and space will dictate the location of a workshop. The most important piece of equipment in the workshop will be the bench, so it is important that any area under consideration should, as a basic requirement, be able to house both you and the bench, as well as allowing space for the furniture being restored. You will also need to surround yourself with tools and machinery, so plan your work area carefully.

YOUR WORKBENCH

Once you have decided where to site your workbench, you will need to assess the various factors that are vital for good work.

The most important factor is the quality of light available. Natural light is ideal, so, if possible, position the bench directly under a window or skylight. Hang fluorescent strip lights above the workbench and, if you are intending to undertake any polishing work, make sure that normal lights are also available (fluorescent light gives a false colour). Also paint the walls white to reflect, and so maximize, whatever light there is.

Rack your tools in an organized manner so that they are readily available. Keep groups of tools, such as hammers, saws or chisels, together for easy access. Keep tools that are not used daily, such as carving tools, carefully wrapped to protect their sharp edges, and stored neatly ready for use. Above all, keep the work area and bench clean and tidy.

Remember that most of your time will be spent standing at the workbench, so put blocks under it, if necessary, to set it at a height that is comfortable for you to work at. Also, if possible, opt for a wooden rather than a concrete floor, as concrete is very tiring on the feet and legs.

If space and funds permit, have two separate areas within the workshop: one for cabinet making and the other, in a dust-free area, for polishing. This dual use maximizes the available space.

An ideal workbench

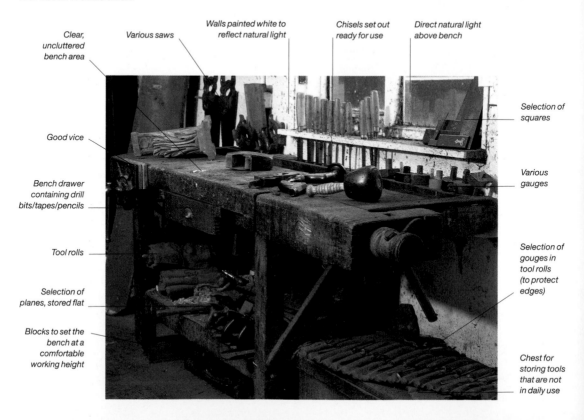

Clear, uncluttered bench area

Various saws

Walls painted white to reflect natural light

Chisels set out ready for use

Direct natural light above bench

Selection of squares

Good vice

Various gauges

Bench drawer containing drill bits/tapes/pencils

Tool rolls

Selection of gouges in tool rolls (to protect edges)

Selection of planes, stored flat

Blocks to set the bench at a comfortable working height

Chest for storing tools that are not in daily use

YOUR TOOLKIT

When restoring antique furniture, the best tools are, without doubt, those that were originally used in the 18th and 19th centuries. For a hobby restorer, modern tools are a suitable, and realistic, substitute, but anyone wishing to pursue a career in the field of furniture restoration should endeavour to build up as wide a collection of antique tools as possible. Such tools were made by craftsmen for craftsmen. The steel used then is still the best for holding a suitable cutting edge now, and the handles, made from box or rosewood, feel more comfortable to the hand than modern materials such as plastic. Often you will see numerous names stamped into the handle of an antique tool, indicating how it has passed through the hands of generations of craftsmen.

Old tools can be found in a number of places, ranging from specialized tool auctions or car boot sales, to local fêtes and classified advertisements in the local paper. If you are really lucky, you may have the opportunity to buy the tools and contents of the workshop of a retiring cabinet-maker. If this happens, beg or borrow the funds to buy the tools, since such events are rare indeed.

In the absence of antique tools, or while you are building up your collection, start your toolkit by buying modern equivalents, but be sure to buy the best quality that is available within your budget. Clamps are an exception to this rule, and modern sash, snap and G-clamps are fine. These are expensive pieces of equipment, so it is a good idea to buy a few whenever you can afford them.

Modern screwdrivers, saws and chisels can be purchased to begin with, and you can gradually replace them with older examples if you want. Some tools and equipment, such as spring clips, can be made in the workshop.

Most cabinet-makers take a lifetime to build up their collection of tools, and almost all craftsmen will prefer to work with only their own tools, which, once purchased, should last a lifetime.

If you become interested in restoring then you may become an avid collector of tools yourself. Certainly, if you decide to take up restoring as a job, then building up your stock of tools and materials can be seen as an investment in your own future. Remember always to respect your tools, keeping them clean and sharp, and wrapping them safely whenever they are not in use.

Safety

The safety rules of a workshop are essentially those of common sense. Always remember that the workshop is potentially a dangerous area, so make sure that children cannot get in. Always handle sharp tools with care and replace them in their rack after use. Keep a regularly tested fire extinguisher close to hand and lock any flammable materials away in a fireproof cabinet. Keep the work area clean and tidy and sweep up all shavings at the end of the day. Good ventilation is important, especially when using stripper or any other chemicals. Make sure any stains or other liquids are kept in jars and clearly labelled. Wear suitable safety clothing as the job dictates. Tie back long hair, remove any dangling jewellery and always wear a long apron to protect your clothes.

Above: *A fire extinguisher is essential. Install a powder-filled fire extinguisher at every exit door.*

Above: *When using power tools likely to create a lot of dust or sparks, it is a good idea to wear a protective helmet.*

Left: *Basic safety equipment should include a first-aid kit, goggles, ear defenders, a filter mask, gloves and a disposable mask.*

SAWS AND MEASURING DEVICES

It is important that saws are kept in good condition because a sharp edge is essential, particularly when doing detailed work. Although modern power saws can take much of the effort out of sawing, and certainly have their place in a workshop, hand-held saws, such as the tenon saw, are invaluable for small-scale work. Measuring devices, including dividers, callipers and gauges, are the key to successful cabinet work, so look after them carefully.

SAWS

The three most commonly used saws in day-to-day restoration are the full tenon saw, the half-tenon saw and the dovetail saw, all of which have varying numbers of teeth per centimetre (inch). The more teeth per centimetre (inch), the finer the cut will be. Some of the finest cutting teeth are those of the fret and coping saws, designed for detailed shape work.

The large panel saw, used for cutting larger boards, comes with two teeth settings: the cross cut, designed to cut across the grain, and the ripsaw, designed to cut along the length of the grain. With the introduction of modern band saws and circular saws, large panel saws are used less frequently, but all workshops should have at least one of each type.

Saws will almost certainly be used on a daily basis and should be used only for the specific task for which they were designed. Using a fine dovetail saw for general work, for example, will damage the teeth and make it unsuitable for the finer work of cutting dovetails.

The saw is a precision cutting tool and should always be kept sharp and in good condition. While it is possible to sharpen the saw yourself, it is far better to send it to a professional saw doctor to have the teeth set and sharpened.

Above: *An extensive range of reliable measuring tools is essential for the furniture restorer to carry out accurate work.*

When using a saw on a particularly difficult piece of wood, rub a little candle wax on the blade to help ease the cutting.

MEASURING DEVICES

"Measure twice, cut once" is an old cabinet-makers' saying, and it is as true today as it has always been. Accurate measuring is vital, since if the measuring is inaccurate then all the work that follows is wasted, at worst possibly leading to a ruined piece of valuable furniture, at best meaning you have to start all over again. Measuring tools include dividers, marking gauges, callipers, set (carpenter's) squares, sliding bevels and box rules, all of which are indispensable. Double-check every measurement and work from a face edge (the first edge cut and planed level, which is then used to take other measurements).

Left: *Three saws from a typical workshop, each with a different number of teeth per centimetre (inch). The more teeth a saw has, the finer the cut will be.*

HAMMERS AND SCREWDRIVERS

Hammers, ranging from pin hammers for light work to heavier hammers for knocking apart furniture, are an essential part of any restoration work, as are the various types of mallet, particularly the carver's dummy, which is a very useful tool. A wide range of screwdrivers should also be kept to hand. Look out for examples with long and short shanks, which are useful in different situations. Be sure to keep the leading edge of a screwdriver sharp.

HAMMERS

The restorer will have two or three different types in the workshop, including the light pin hammer, the general cabinet hammer, which will be used on a daily basis, and a heavier hammer used to knock apart carcasses and drive in large nails. Hammers should never be used to hit another tool, such as a chisel – that is exclusively the role of the mallet.

When the face of a hammer becomes dirty and worn, file it flat then rub it lightly with fine-grade sandpaper to remove the dirt and score the surface. This enables the hammer to grip the head of the nail. This process, which is known as "dressing", will probably need to be done at least two or three times a month.

MALLETS

These were designed to be used against the handle of a tool such as a chisel or gouge. They come in different weights and shapes, and the greater the weight of the head, the more force it will exert. A good example of this is the carver's dummy, whose heavy lignum vitae head

Above: *Two traditional mallets – it is useful to have a selection in your workshop.*

ensures that a simple wrist action gives a very strong blow. It also means that the carver need not look at the mallet as it swings down, since its rounded head will always strike the tool being used, thus allowing the carver to concentrate fully on the work in hand.

Larger mallets are for roughing off, while lighter ones are for delicate work. The square-headed mallet is for general cabinet work and knocking apart, where a large hammer might bruise the wood.

SCREWDRIVERS

It is best to equip yourself with as wide a range of screwdrivers as possible. It is well worth spending a little time at car boot sales or trawling through second-hand shops in order to build a collection of traditional tools at a lower price than new ones. Old screwdrivers tend to have a longer shank, which gives better leverage. They also have handles made from box-wood or beech, which are kinder to the hand than plastic. Small screwdrivers with short shanks can be very useful for removing screws in awkward locations.

When buying an old screwdriver, check that the leading edge is straight and even. If it is worn or uneven, you will have to grind it flush, because a screwdriver that does not fit snugly into a screw-head slot can break the screw. Remember that a screwdriver is designed for removing and putting in screws and should never be used as a lever, which could damage the edge and bend the shank.

Below: *A selection of old screwdrivers with shanks of varying lengths.*

Holding a hammer

1 *When using a hammer, the most common mistake is to hold it half way down the handle in the belief that this allows more control and accuracy. In fact, it has the opposite effect.*

2 *The correct way to hold the hammer is at the end of its handle, which gives much better balance and control. When using a hammer, make several medium blows rather than trying to drive the nail home first time.*

SMOOTHING TOOLS AND CLAMPS

There are many different types of planes and clamps used in restoration work, and modern tools are very similar to their traditional counterparts. Some planes are fitted with their own guide fences and others with changeable blades, while moulding planes have specially shaped bases and blades for detailed shaping work. Different clamps, like planes, are designed for particular tasks and it is advisable to build up as wide a selection as possible.

PLANES

The earliest planes were made with wood bodies, but during the 18th and 19th centuries the metal-bodied plane took over, although the moulding planes remained wooden.

There are various examples of planes, each suited to a particular role, including the utilitarian jack plane, the smoothing plane, and the smaller block-and-shoulder plane for more intricate work. There are also specialized planes, such as moulding planes, with their specially shaped bases and blades, which are designed to cut the waist, base and other mouldings found on carcass furniture. However, the modern router, with its wide range of shaped cutters, has largely taken over this role. Although the spokeshave does not look like a plane, it is classed as one because it works along the same principle.

The blade of any plane is designed to cut the wood cleanly without tearing the grain, and so it is important that it is always kept sharp. When the blade is sharp and the plane is used correctly, it should made a wonderful slicing sound as it cuts through the wood.

SCRAPERS

The cabinet scraper, which is basically a piece of metal with a burred edge, is designed to clean up surfaces and remove any plane marks prior to sanding.

The most frequently used scraper will be a rectangular one for shaped mouldings, but tailor-made scrapers are also useful. The most common example is the French curve, which is shaped like a kidney and should be able to scrape any concave area.

Scrapers should always be used sharp and should produce shavings, not dust. To sharpen a scraper, you should draw a hard piece of rounded metal, such as the shank of a screwdriver, across the edge. This produces a burr, which is needed to cut the wood.

SANDING EQUIPMENT

The earliest types of sandpaper were, in fact, made from sharkskin, known as shagreen. It was dried and used very much in the same way as sandpaper is today. This was followed by the use of ground glass or sand, which was stuck to paper, and it is from this that the terms "glasspaper" and "sandpaper" are derived.

Nowadays there are many abrasive papers available, including silicon carbide, aluminium oxide and garnet paper, but the term "sandpaper" is still commonly used to describe them all. These papers are available in a number of different grits, or grades, with the most commonly used grits in the workshop ranging from 80 (the coarsest) to 320 (the finest).

Sandpaper is rarely used on its own but is wrapped around sanding blocks of cork or wood. If a specific moulding has to be sanded, you will need to make a shaped piece of wood (overloe) that matches the profile of the moulding, so that it can be sanded without having its shape altered. Over the years, the restorer will build up a wide selection of tailor-made overloes.

When you start sandpapering a piece of work, begin with the coarsest grade and work up through the grades to the finest. Wetting the wood between each grade, and allowing it to dry before you start with the next grade, will give a smoother finish. Also, if you intend to apply a water stain, this inter-grade wetting process will make sure that the grain does not rise at the staining stage.

Above: *A selection of planes showing some of the variety of shapes and materials used in their construction.*

Above: *The spokeshave is a cross between a plane and a scraper, and is a very versatile tool for shaping wood.*

Above: *Overloes are specially shaped wooden blocks that are used with sandpaper to smooth the profile of a moulding.*

CLAMPS

These tools come in a wide variety of styles, each suited to a particular role. The most common types are the long sash clamp, the G-clamp, which comes in different sizes, the band clamp, the snap clamp and the spring clip. Modern clamps are similar to traditional ones, and although they are fairly expensive to buy, it is best to have as wide a range as possible.

When working with clamps, always use clamping blocks to prevent bruising and the appearance of "hoof" marks on the wood. Also, never over-tighten a clamp: the pressure it exerts can cause structural damage to delicate pieces.

When gluing up a complex job, it is a good idea to have a "dry" run beforehand, working out which clamps will be used and in which order. Spending a little time doing this may prevent problems later on

when the glue has been applied and is setting. It also means that you will have everything you need to hand and will feel confident about starting the work.

Above: *A wide selection of modern and traditional clamps, including G-clamps and sash clamps, are essential for many types of restoration work.*

Making a band clamp

While most clamps can be bought, the steel band clamp is unique in that it is workshop made and tailored to a particular job in hand. Its role is to clamp an oval or round, creating an equal pressure around the circumference.

You will need a small block of hardwood, a steel band (as used for binding building materials), small screws and a clamp.

1 *Cut two lengths of the steel band to a length slightly shorter than the frame's circumference and punch two pilot holes into each end of them.*

2 *Using a metal bit, drill two small holes through the pilot holes. Be sure to place a scrap block of wood on the bench or worktop to protect it.*

3 *Use a countersink drill bit to countersink the two holes previously drilled. This will make sure that the screw heads are level with the band.*

4 *After marking the shape of the frame on the hardwood, use a band saw to cut the concave profile. Cut the block in half.*

5 *Screw the two lengths of steel band to the shaped side of the hardwood, making sure that the countersunk hole side of the band is used.*

6 *Finish by filing the screw heads flush with the metal band, this will make sure that no unnecessary scratching or marking occurs.*

7 *The band clamp in use. The hardwood blocks are clamped together to create the tension.*

CHISELS AND CARVING TOOLS

All these implements have their own jobs, which involve paring away wood in one form or another, but one rule applicable to all is to keep their edges sharp so that they can cut through wood and not tear the grain. If you are interested in carving, you will start to amass a large collection of tools, since each has its own specific function. In general, old examples tend to keep their edge longer than modern versions, due to the better-quality steel.

CHISELS

The cabinet-maker or restorer will have three main types of chisel to hand on the workbench. These are the paring chisel, the mortise chisel and the firmer chisel. Within these groupings there should be a range of widths suitable for any task.

The paring chisel, with its bevelled edges and long blade, is primarily used for paring, levelling and chamfering. It is designed for hand-use only and should never be struck with a mallet.

The mortise chisel, as its name suggests, is used to cut out mortises, and for this reason its blade is noticeably thicker than that of both the paring and firmer chisels. The thickness of the blade means that it can withstand a heavy blow from a mallet and a certain amount of leverage when removing the waste wood from a mortise.

The firmer chisel, with its shorter, thicker blade without a bevelled side, is designed for heavier work and can be used in conjunction with a suitable mallet.

CARVING TOOLS

The carver is one of the most skilled craftspeople in the field of antique restoration. The skill of carving is similar to that of a painter, except that the carver's medium is wood and the end results are three-dimensional.

The required tools, which can number into the thousands, are known individually for their suitabilities and strengths, and before undertaking a carving project the carver will select the required implements and sharpen them. Indeed, depending on the hardness of the wood, it is not unknown for a carver to resharpen a blade every few minutes during carving work.

Small carving tools are essential for detailed and intricate work. They provide much greater control of the task in hand, allowing the carver to remove small slivers of wood with the minimum of effort.

There are numerous types of carving tools, including scrolls, which set out the shape of the carving; V- or parting tools, which produce long sweeps; grounders,

Above: *While gradually building up a collection of antique tools, which you can find in second-hand shops, it is a good idea to purchase modern equivalents too.*

which remove the background waste; veiners, which carve the fine details, such as flowers, leaves, etc; and fish tails, which, like the grounders, help to remove unwanted wood.

While this procedure may seem very complicated, it is worth noting that the complexity and intricacy of much of the work means that it takes several years for a carver to reach full potential.

Each carving project can often take hundreds of hours of painstaking work, and, aside from patience, the main skill a potential carver needs to learn is the ability to be able to study an existing carving closely and to mimic exactly the hand in which it was originally carved. The real test of the master carver is to restore carving to the extent that the new work blends in seamlessly with the original detail.

Left: *A selection of chisels, gouges and bradawls (for making fine pilot holes) will be used on a daily basis.*

Left: *A small selection of the many hundreds of carving tools required by the master carver.*

Above: *A carver's vice allows free and easy access to any carved piece held in it.*

Sharpening a chisel

Some of the tools most used by the cabinet-maker or furniture restorer are the various chisels. These are used to pare, level and shape the wood. It is vital that the chisels are kept sharp at all times, as failure to do so will result in them tearing the grain rather than slicing through the wood. When a chisel loses its edge, the process of re-honing takes only a few minutes, and the procedure is very simple.

1 *Using a grinding wheel and selecting the finest grade of the two stones, offer the chisel at an angle of approximately 25–30 degrees. Remove the bevel as soon as it is flat, otherwise the chisel's length will be shortened too much and its working life substantially reduced.*

2 *Lightly lubricate an oil stone with a fine oil, then draw the chisel repeatedly along the stone at an angle of 30–35 degrees. This will produce the cutting edge.*

3 *Turn the chisel over and lay it flat down on the stone. Rub it back and forth two or three times. This process, known as "backing off", will weaken the burr that has built up. Strop the chisel on a piece of leather, which should remove the burr.*

4 *Finally, use your newly sharpened chisel to cut a slither off a piece of wood. This will check for sharpness as well as removing the burr, should it not have come off on the leather strop.*

5 *The illustration shows how the finished edge should look if the chisel has been sharpened correctly.*

TURNING TOOLS

Since medieval times, turning has been used in the construction of furniture. While lathes have changed with the times – the earliest examples were human-powered – the basic techniques and principles used by the early bodgers (travelling lathe craftsmen) have remained much the same as they are today. Likewise, the tools used in modern workshops would still be recognizable to the turner of centuries past.

The tools of the turner are divided into measuring and turning tools. It is vital that accuracy is maintained, and this is done with the aid of the measuring tools: dividers to measure length and width and callipers to measure external or internal dimensions. Both take measurements from a template (pattern) and can be used easily when the lathe is in operation.

The turning tools, which have long blades and long handles to counteract the force of the lathe, are divided into four groups. First there are the gouges, which are used to rough off the wood to an approximate cylinder. Next are the skew chisels, used to refine the shape of the cylinder to its final form. The scrapers are used to make the grooves and turnings, and finally the parting tools are used to form long trenches and part the turnings from the waste wood.

Due to the stresses imposed on the tools they should be kept sharp and constantly checked for any possible stress fractures. This is one of the occasions when it is preferable for the restorer to use modern tools rather than their antique

equivalents. This is because the latter may have developed stress factors in their blades or faults in their handles, which, if fractured during application, could cause serious injury to the turner. It is also important, therefore, to make sure that the tools are always used correctly. Due to the potential risks involved when using a

Above: *A wide selection of measuring and turning tools is necessary to ensure that all turned work is accurate.*

lathe, it is essential to take an approved instructional course in turning before beginning lathe work (see Further Information, p.95).

Left: *The tap and die is a turning tool that is at the opposite end of the spectrum to high-speed lathes.*

Right: *Turning tools are distinctively different from woodworking chisels.*

Cutting a male screw thread

When turning and cutting a new thread, it is important to make sure that both male and female parts are of a corresponding size. As dies (internally threaded tools for cutting male threads) and screw taps (threaded steel cylinders for cutting female threads) exist in corresponding pairs, a match should be found. Remember that once you have started cutting, you must continue working until the thread is finished; stopping and starting will mean that you will not get a perfect match.

1 *Select and cut a piece of wood that is slightly larger in width than the diameter of the thread that is being replaced.*

2 *Turn the wood with a large gouge. Measure the size of the die housing using callipers, then compare this measurement to the size of the turned wood.*

3 *Turn the column to the final diameter required, checking the measurements with the callipers as you work.*

4 *Place the turned column in the vice and, using a sharp chisel, cut a leading edge in the column. This will aid the beginning of the thread cutting.*

5 *Place the die, which has an inset cutting blade, on top of the turned column. Start turning it in a clockwise direction to cut the thread.*

6 *Keeping the die level, follow the technique of one full rotation clockwise followed by one half rotation counterclockwise. This clears the blade of shavings.*

7 *Continue all the way to the base and then remove the die. Remove the wood column and cut it to the required length.*

Cutting a female screw thread

A corresponding female thread now needs to be cut to match the male thread. Should the female and male threads be of different sizes, a solution is to plug the female thread with a suitable piece of wood and then recut the female wood to a size to correspond with the male thread.

1 *Place a piece of wood in a vice. Drill a corresponding hole into it of compatible size to the turned male thread, then pare a leading edge on the hole with a sharp chisel.*

2 *Grip the screw tap in the vice and place the leading edge on top of it. Turn the piece of wood one complete turn clockwise followed by a half turn counterclockwise.*

3 *When completed, the male and female parts should fit snugly together and the thread should work with ease.*

MACHINERY

While antique restoration is traditionally a craft that relies on hand-held tools, the use of machinery can, in certain cases, make life much easier. It was the mass introduction of mechanized tools during the 19th century that radically altered furniture production. Although they can never replace the trained craftsman, the new generation of hand-held power tools available today will certainly save you many valuable hours in the workshop.

The use of heavy machinery in the restoration workshop is fairly limited. In fact, not many restoration workshops will have the space for a fully fitted machine shop, especially as the heavier types often require three-phase electricity supplies. (This involves installing a unit to boost the power from single to three phase, and is usually needed only in commercial workshops.) However, the inclusion of certain heavy machines can make life much easier, and two invaluable machines are the band saw and the lathe.

Hand-held machine tools, such as an electric or cordless drill, jigsaw and router, are a great help, and you should stock as wide a range of router cutters as possible. You could also buy a router bench, which extends the possibilities of the router. As finances and space allow, you can buy extra machinery, such as circular saws, thickness planers and pillar drills.

While these will not be used on a daily basis, they can save hours of effort when they are required. As with all machinery, it is vital that you obtain the correct training before using it (see Further Information, p.95) and that you always carefully follow the safety instructions.

BAND SAW

The band saw's blade is a flexible length of steel that runs in a continuous loop. It is ideal for cutting curves and angles or for trimming strips from wider pieces. Its limitations are governed by the depth of the sawbed and the thickness of the blade. Never apply undue pressure to the blade, as this will damage it or the guiding rollers and cause it to snap.

As a general rule, allow the saw to cut at its own speed. Any excessive force will be indicated by the driving motors straining and starting to slow down.

band saw

lathe

LATHE

The lathe allows you to accomplish a wide variety of tasks, ranging from the turning of legs, bobbins, bead mouldings and spindles to the copying of handles and decorative roundels or paterae.

Due to the speed and torque at which lathes operate, a lathe with a heavy cast body is ideal for restoration work, as this will counter any vibration. It is essential to take an approved instructional course in lathe work before you start using one as misuse can result in serious injury.

router

router bench

jigsaw

electric drill

cordless drill

ROUTER

The router is an extremely versatile hand tool. Its shaped cutter rotates at high speeds and will, if used correctly, give a clean, even cut. It can also be used with a guide fence or depth stop, and the range of cutters available is immense. Care should be taken in its use: no loose clothing should be worn, hair should be tied back and eye protection should be worn.

ROUTER BENCH

The router bench allows the router to be mounted upside down and so converted into a spindle moulder. The bench should always be used with guide fences and safety guards. The bench can often be dismantled, allowing for convenient storage when not in use.

POWER DRILLS

Cordless and electric drills are both ideal machines for workshop use. While you may sometimes require the use of a more traditional hand drill, such as when undertaking delicate work that may need to be executed one turn of the drill bit at a time, a power drill is one of the few modern tools that is preferred over the old version.

Always buy the best model possible and, in the case of a cordless drill, always have the spare battery on charge ready to be changed over. These drills can also be used with screwdriver heads, although this would, of course, be for more general use and not for fine antique work, since the brass and steel antique screw heads would break if a power drill were used on them. Both types of drill can be used with a variety of bits and will accomplish a multitude of tasks. A drill stand can also be purchased to allow the drill to be used as a pillar drill.

JIGSAW

The jigsaw has a blade with a rise and fall action that cuts through sheet wood with ease. While it is not suitable for fine work, it is ideal for roughing out or cutting shaped templates (patterns) when the pieces are too large to fit into a band saw. Remember that the blade passes through the wood and continues to cut below, so care should be taken when using this tool.

COLLECTING AND STORING WOOD

A supply of suitable wood is an essential aspect of a restorer's workshop, and different kinds must be sourced, collected and properly stored. To the casual observer, such a collection of pieces of wood, salvaged from previous centuries of furniture making, may seem little more than firewood, but to the antique furniture restorer they are a priceless commodity, as without them his or her task would be impossible to undertake.

The aim of every restorer is, wherever possible, to restore a piece of furniture without trace. To do this requires the use of old surface woods and veneers that match the original as closely as possible in colour and grain. Also, when missing mouldings have to be remade, the material used must be of the same type as the original in order to make a good repair.

Two woods in constant demand by restorers are Cuban and Honduras mahogany, which, during the 18th century, were the woods of choice for furniture making. Both are now nearly impossible to buy from any wood merchant, and so any old examples found must be bought and put away until needed. This shows the vital importance of the restorer's "breaker store".

The breaker store, as the name so graphically describes, is a collection of pieces of antique furniture that have been bought not to be restored but to be carefully knocked apart, sorted into the various woods and stacked away for future reuse in the restoration of better pieces. Such an example might be a collection of quarter-sawn oak drawer sides, waiting to be used in the repair or replacement of a missing drawer, or perhaps an old Cuban mahogany table leaf, long ago separated from its table, waiting to be used in the making of a missing bracket foot or to be reshaped with a moulding plane to replace a missing section of top moulding.

The source of breakers is endless, and no opportunity should be missed to scour junk shops, local auctions or even skips. An old Victorian chest bought for very little indeed could provide enough oak linings, Cuban mahogany and even old locks to pay for itself many times over. Building a comprehensive breaker store can be a lifetime's work, and a useful tip to keep a store expanding is that every time some wood is used from the store, it should be replaced with more wood than was taken out. Indeed, it is a prerequisite for application to the antique restorers' most senior trade organization, The British Antique Furniture Restorers' Association (BAFRA), that the applicant is able to demonstrate the active building-up of a collection of breakers.

Right: A well-stocked and logically arranged breaker store will supply a restorer with wood to match virtually any restoration project.

The breaker store should be racked and labelled and the woods stored in the various marked sections. This saves both time and effort when searching for a particular piece and enables the restorer to see which, if any, types of veneer are running low or are not represented at all.

Any veneers should be removed from their wood core and stored separately in a veneer store. Any nails and screws should also be removed, partly for potential reuse if they are in good condition and partly as a method of preventing any unnecessary scratching from occurring. The store should be kept dry but not overly so, as

excessive heat will cause the woods to warp and split, creating as many problems as dampness.

While the majority of woods will be old, if an opportunity arises it is a good idea to buy some modern woods, such as walnut, yew or oak for renovating country-made pieces. These should then be professionally cut into boards, stacked so that air can circulate freely between them and allowed to dry and season naturally under cover.

If, however, space will not allow this storage, and modern wood has to be purchased when needed, remember that

it is always better to buy air-dried rather than kiln-dried wood, as the former will be more stable in the long term.

To the untrained eye, a restorer's breaker store may look like a confused jumble of wood. The owner, however, will know all the stock that is there, even wood that was acquired years ago. When a particular grain or surface is needed, the restorer should be able to locate it almost immediately, recalling it from the day it was placed there. Next to tools, an extensive and expanding supply of breakers is one of the most important considerations for a furniture restorer.

Below: *An example of the numerous repairs for which the components of a breaker chest can be used.*

Veneer used for patching small areas of damaged or missing veneer

Solid mahogany sides used for making bracket feet, mouldings etc

Handles and locks used as replacements for missing ones

Oak drawer sides used for replacement sides or damaged drawers

Old surface pine from carcass used for patching old surfaces etc

POLISHES AND GLUES

One of the most attractive features of antique furniture is its distinctive grain patterns. It is the application of polish and waxes that, while helping to protect, feed and nourish the wood, also enhances its appearance.

The polishes and techniques used today are nearly identical to those used for generations before, although the restorers of old would have had to make their own polish recipes as well as making all their own glues.

POLISHES

Ever since wooden furniture was first made, its grain has been sealed in one way or another. Waxes were used to burnish the surface, and, during the 17th century, varnishes were applied that helped to protect and enhance the wood. During the 19th century, a new technique was adopted that resulted in a shellac polish, made from the shells of lac beetles, being applied with a cotton and linen pad known as a rubber (see pp.39–40). This sealed the grain, protected the wood and brought out the pattern and figure of popular imported woods such as mahogany, satinwood and rosewood.

The polisher's basic requirements are few. The equipment involves wadding (batting) and linen or other lint-free cloth for making rubbers, a selection of various grades of wire (steel) wool, as well as a wide selection of various brushes and some mutton cloth for buffing surfaces.

The polisher's materials include shellac polish, which can be bought in either liquid form or as shellac flakes to be

mixed with spirit (alcohol), and is kept in a glass or plastic bottle. Various coloured pigments to be mixed with water or spirit are needed for tinting or colouring repairs, and stopping waxes, again in various shades, are also needed. The final material is methylated spirits (methyl alcohol), which should be stored in a fire-proof cabinet. All the above equipment and materials can be obtained from a good trade supplier.

One of the main attractions of an antique piece of furniture is its colour and, hopefully, its patinated surface, so great care should be taken whenever polish is applied. The skill of the polisher is to revive a surface by gently removing the perished layers and then rebuilding the surface layer by layer. Work on small areas should be kept as localized as possible so as not to affect the surrounding areas.

Above: *Brushes, polishes and stains are needed for nearly every restoration job. Keep a good selection to hand.*

Patience and practice are therefore the watchwords. A good eye for colour is also needed to ensure that patches and repairs blend in with the surroundings areas. They should be practically invisible. It is also essential to have an understanding of traditional techniques and materials and to know when to clean a piece and when it is better to leave it alone. Over-zealous cleaning will not only spoil the aesthetic appearance but will almost certainly devalue the piece considerably.

Professionally, a polisher may take many years to learn the craft, and, without doubt, the polisher's role in a workshop is every bit as important as that of the cabinet-maker or restorer.

Above: *Rubbers should be kept in an air-tight jar or tin to stop them drying out.*

GLUES

Until the 15th and early 16th centuries, very little glue was used in the manufacture of furniture. Instead, the joints were held together with pegs or crude, hand-made clout nails. By the 17th century, however, as furniture construction became more complex and designs and styles more adventurous, animal glues were being employed in furniture making.

While new adhesives have been developed over the years, animal glues are still the most frequently used glues in furniture restoration. The sight and smell of the glue pot in any workshop is the same today as it was in the 17th, 18th and 19th centuries, and putting it on the fire or hot plate is still the apprentice's first task every morning.

Three main types of glue are used in the modern workshop: animal glue, PVA (white) glue and cascamite. Each has its own role and will be selected according to the nature of the required join.

Animal glue

This glue is made today as it has been for the last 300 years: animal feet and skin are boiled and the resulting liquid is poured into cold water, causing it to crystallize into small pearls. These pearls can then be mixed with water and allowed to soak overnight, before being heated in a special glue pot to melt them.

Above: *Animal glue is applied hot, using a bristle brush.*

Above: *The three most commonly used glues today (clockwise from top): animal glue, PVA (white) glue and cascamite.*

The glue pot (or gesso kettle) is an iron bain-marie pot with an inner reservoir of hot water. The pot is put on a fire or hotplate until the water boils, and it is then allowed to simmer gently, melting the glue ready for use. A top crust will appear and should be scraped off prior to use.

Great care should be taken not to allow the hot-water reservoir to boil dry. Should this happen, the glue will become too hot and its adhesive qualities will be lost. The remaining glue will then have to be discarded and a new batch prepared.

At the end of each day, the glue pot is taken off the heat and set aside until the next day, when it is simply reheated and the glue reused. A pot of glue could be cooled and then reheated day after day, but it is good workshop practice to make a fresh batch of animal glue every week.

Animal glue is ideal for furniture restoration because it allows a certain flexibility in the joints, it can be removed with hot water or spirit (alcohol) and it sets as soon as it has cooled. It can also be watered down to make a size for use on veneers and surfaces when a piece of furniture needs re-veneering.

The disadvantages of animal glue, however, are that it is affected by extremes of heat and cold and that a sharp blow to a joint will cause it to lose its adhesion. If such a break happens, the joint has to be taken apart, cleaned and reglued. Despite these disadvantages, however, no serious workshop would be without its glue pot.

Above: *Animal glues are heated prior to use in an iron bain-marie pot. The water reservoir should not be allowed to boil dry.*

PVA glue

Another frequently used glue is the more modern polyvinylacetate, or PVA (white), glue. It is bought in liquid form, is easy to use, needs no pre-application preparation and is unaffected by either extreme of temperature. The joint or two surfaces being joined must be brought under pressure when the glue (which is non-reversible) is applied.

When it is either impractical to have a glue pot simmering away all day, or when you are doing a small restoration job that simply does not warrant the time involved in preparing animal glue, versatile and simple-to-use PVA is the ideal workshop adhesive.

Cascamite

For projects needing an adhesive that will help to hold a shape or form, an ideal glue is urea-formaldehyde resin, or cascamite as it is more commonly known. This comes in a powder form and is mixed with water to a creamy paste. Once the glue has been applied, the two surfaces being joined should be brought under pressure with suitable clamps.

Cascamite is a versatile glue: its natural white colour can be disguised by adding coloured pigments to it, and some types are waterproof, which can be useful. The disadvantage, however, is that it is very brittle when set, making it totally unsuitable for joints, because just a knock could shatter the glue bond.

STAINS

The restorer today commonly uses stains, which can be based on water, oil or spirit, to help disguise a repair. However, stains had another use during the 17th and 18th centuries. They were applied to enhance timbers and to give them a more exotic appearance: for example, pearwood was stained black to resemble the more sought after and expensive ebony, and sycamore was stained green to give chairs a more vibrant look.

The majority of coloured stains are either water- or spirit- (alcohol-) based, although on rare occasions a slow-drying, oil-based stain may be used. They are used to colour in repairs or to help colour out and disguise marks. Some stains can be bought in liquid form, but for the best range of tones and colours you will need to buy stains in powder form, ready to be mixed with spirit or water.

Spirit-based stains, usually mixed with methylated spirits (methyl alcohol), are quick-drying, which makes them unsuitable for use on large areas, as some areas will dry before others, causing an uneven finish. Spirit stains are usually applied after polishing. If the polish is applied on top of the stain, the spirit in the polish will dilute the stain and lighten the surface colour.

Water-based stains dry more slowly, making them suitable for large areas because they give an even finish. They are generally applied before polishing. One disadvantage, however, is that they can

Left: *Stains often have to be tailor-made to suit the job in hand.*

raise the grain, which will then need to be flattened before you can proceed any further. Both spirit and water stains can be thinned after application by adding further spirit/water.

Other stains, such as coloured waxes, are not frequently used in furniture restoration. Their use is generally confined to moderating the colour of a surface slightly after it has been polished.

Stains can be applied by brush, which should be thoroughly cleaned after use, with a cloth or by a dowel with some cloth wrapped around the end, known as a swab (see p.42). Alternatively, some polish can be mixed with a small amount of stain and applied with a fad. This allows the whole area to be slightly tinted, and it overcomes the problem of the spirit base lightening the colour.

Mixing a spirit-based stain

1 Aways use a clean container and a flat-bladed knife or small teaspoon for mixing stains. Methylated spirits (methyl alcohol) is an ideal spirit liquid mixer.

2 Pour the required quantity of methylated spirits into the clean container. It is better to add powder to liquid rather than liquid to powder, in order to avoid unnecessary wastage. Select the correct powder required for the colour effect desired, and add a small amount at a time.

3 Mix with a clean brush. If a stronger stain tone is needed, simply add further powder. When you have finished with the stain, pour away the unused stain and clean all the utensils and the brush to ensure that the next coloured stain to be mixed is not tinted with any residue from this one.

UPHOLSTERY

Most restorers are more than competent to remove and undertake basic upholstery, but the actual skill of upholstering antique furniture to a good standard is a qualified trade that will take a number of years of training to master. An understanding of the methods and techniques used in upholstery is, however, essential and, like a general knowledge of leathering, will give the restorer a better understanding of his or her craft.

The tools for upholstery fall into two categories: those for removing existing upholstery and those for reupholstery. Styles and techniques vary from country to country.

For example, in Britain and the USA the upholstered piece is raised on a bench or trestles and the upholsterer stands, while in France the general practice is to work with the piece on the floor and the upholsterer on his or her knees. Also, due to the fashion for French furniture being more rounded, especially on the edges, rounded needles are used to stitch rolled edges, while the English method, with its preference for a neater, more precise edge, requires the use of a longer, straighter needle for the stitching.

Occasionally hay has been used to stuff the seat, but horsehair is more common. Horsehair, however, is becoming increasingly difficult to source, and pigs' hair is often being used in its place. Commercial upholstery workshops will try to buy second-hand horsehair mattresses, which give a good supply of hair that can be carded (teased

out) and reused. Synthetic hair is another alternative, but given the choice most qualified upholsterers prefer natural hair. Another innovation is the staple gun, which is sometimes used to secure fabric instead of upholstery tacks.

Cushions should be filled with traditional down feathers rather than modern synthetic materials, which lack the weight and feel of the original. Traditionally, the down was stuffed into a

Above: *A selection of materials, including horse hair, webbing and springs, needed for reupholstering furniture.*

goatskin suede bag around which the finish fabric was applied. This made sure that the down did not work itself through the fabric. Today, a waxed cotton jacket is adequate for the purpose. In the case of the thinner squab seats for dining chairs, good quality foam is acceptable should rubberized horsehair, which is bought in sheet form, be unavailable.

There are two types of webbing technique: stuff-over and underwebbing. Stuff-over gives a harder, flatter line and was used on English upholstered furniture from the 17th century onward. Continental upholsterers often favoured underwebbing, used in conjunction with internal springs, which gives a more rounded appearance. Certain styles or periods of chair may suit one method of webbing more than the other, but both are acceptable.

Left: *The variety of coverings and trims available is extensive.*

Restoration techniques

Of all the types of furniture, chairs often endure a hard life, which can take a toll on their structure. Over the years, the joints become weakened, fine-shaped backs and legs can suffer from breaks, delicate carving can be damaged or lost and upholstery will become worn or simply out of style.

DISMANTLING AND REASSEMBLING CHAIRS

Learning how to dismantle and reassemble chairs is an important skill for the furniture restorer. One of the most common problems in chairs is loose joints, and the easiest way to rectify this problem is to dismantle the whole chair, reglue the joints and reassemble the chair. Other damage, such as to the frames and backs of chairs, may require a chair to be dismantled only partly before the restorer can start to put the problem right.

Removing upholstery

Upholstery often sustains the most damage and may need to be replaced, in which case it can be removed in the quickest possible way without regard for any damage that it may suffer. If, however, the upholstery is in good condition, it should be removed carefully so that it can be replaced once the frame has been repaired.

The upholstery on this single Regency dining chair is in good condition, but it must be removed so that the damage to the back can be repaired. A careful and methodical approach must be employed to ensure that the upholstery is not damaged and remains in a suitable condition to be reused, if wished.

MATERIALS AND EQUIPMENT	
• tack remover	• pincers
• heavy mallet	• utility knife
• ripping chisel	
• narrow, flat-bladed tool	

1 Place the chair upside down on a protected workbench (a blanket can be spread over it) and remove the tacks from the dust cover with a tack remover and heavy mallet. The latter is used because its weight will ensure that a gentle wrist action will knock out the tacks. Work along the grain, not across it, to avoid splitting the seat rail.

2 Decorative braid is often held in place by glue and a few gimp pins, as is the case here. Remove the pins with a ripping chisel,then pull the braid off. Alternatively, the braid may simply be glued on. If the chair is close-nailed, the nails can easily be knocked out with a tack remover and mallet.

3 Turn the chair on to its side to remove the top cover. Handle the fabric carefully because it may be refitted after the chair is repaired. Remove the upholstery tacks with a tack remover, as in step 1, and remove any staples by slipping a narrow, flat-bladed tool between the staples and frame to lift them, before pulling them out with pincers.

4 With the top cover removed, you can detach the various layers of material and stuffing from the seat. Do this with a tack remover and a heavy mallet. If necessary, remove each layer separately. You may need to use a utility knife to cut through some of the layers of upholstery.

5 Once you have removed all the tacks, lift away the top cover. Keep the horsehair and other stuffing materials safely together.

6 Finally, remove and discard the webbings. These will often be attached with the largest tacks found on the chair, which will require strong blows with the mallet. Make sure that the chair is secure on the bench; if possible, ask someone to hold it for you.

Knocking the chair apart

The majority of restoration techniques, regardless of the style or type of chair, will require the chair to be partially or completely dismantled. As the term "knocking apart" suggests, the chair will be taken to pieces with the aid of a mallet and/or hammer. This should be done with care and patience, however, to make sure that further damage is not caused in the process. The frame of this chair is in quite good condition, so care must be taken when knocking it apart to ensure that no damage is caused to the joints.

MATERIALS AND EQUIPMENT
- masking tape
- pincers
- hardwood block
- hammer
- screwdriver
- drill
- wood drill bit
- metal drill bit

1 First, label all the parts of the chair. With a single chair, the various components will be obvious. If more than one chair is being repaired at the same time, however, parts can easily be confused, causing a major problem when you try to reassemble them.

2 Check to see if the corner blocks have been nailed to the frame. If they have, remove the nails with pincers. Once the nails are removed, or if no nails were used, place a block of hardwood against each corner block in turn to protect it from bruising, and give a firm hammer blow. Remove the blocks.

3 Next, unscrew any metal brackets. These are often found where a chair has been broken and repaired in the past. While these solve a problem in the short term, at a later stage the repaired joint will work itself loose again.

▷

Knocking the chair apart...continued

Tip

If a joint is particularly tight, it may help to inject methylated spirits (methyl alcohol) into it. This will soften the glue and aid dismantling.

4 Make a quick inspection of the chair to look for any tenon pegs and screws that may have been put through the mortise and tenon joints to strengthen them. If you find any, drill them out.

5 Knock the side seat rails apart from the back uprights. Lift the back clear of the workbench and apply a series of firm blows to the back near the joints, protecting the uprights with the hardwood block.

6 Follow the same process with the other seat-rail joints at the front of the chair. If some joints are very tight and cannot be knocked apart without causing damage, try the Tip (top right) or leave them as they are.

7 Finally, knock the back seat rail, back support and top rail away from the back upright. Note that for many chair repairs the knocking apart can stop before this stage, with the back left intact.

8 Once the chair is knocked apart, double-check that all the components are present before you begin restoration work.

Reassembling the chair

Once any necessary repair work has been undertaken, the chair can be reassembled. While chairs come in various styles, shapes and woods, the steps necessary to reassemble them remain fairly consistent. The process of gluing the chair joints together during reassembly will cure many problems, such as wobbly legs and creaking.

MATERIALS AND EQUIPMENT
- toothbrush
- rasp or file
- PVA (white) glue
- sash clamps
- clamping blocks
- gauge sticks
- hardwood block
- hammer

▷ **1** Clean all the joints using either a toothbrush and hot water, which will dissolve the animal glue, or, if this is not successful, a rasp or file. Be careful to remove only the old glue and not any of the wood itself, because any reduction in tenon thickness results in a sloppy joint.

2 Glue the front legs and seat rail together and secure them with a sash clamp and clamping blocks. Check that the legs are parallel by measuring the gap at the top and bottom. Leave to dry overnight.

3 Glue the back uprights together, making sure the back support is inserted at the same time as the back seat rail. As with the front legs, ensure that the uprights are parallel. Clamp to secure and leave to dry overnight.

4 Remove the sash clamps and fit the side seat rails to hold the chair together. Stand the chair on a flat surface while doing this to ensure that it sits level and does not rock. Apply sash clamps.

◁ **5** Before the glue is dry, check that the seat frame is square by comparing both diagonals with pointed gauge sticks held firmly together. If any adjustment is needed, loosen the clamps, ease the joint(s) slightly, retighten the clamps, then check again.

▷ **6** When the glue has dried, add the corner blocks, tapping them lightly into place and using a block of wood to prevent bruising. Leave the sash clamps in place while doing this to make sure that the tapping does not loosen the joint.

7 Now you can fit the back top rail. This chair has sliding dovetails for the joints, and so the top rail is fitted last. In chairs where the back top rail is mortised and tenoned, however, it should be fitted when the two back uprights are glued together.

8 Clamp the bowed back in place under light pressure, using clamping blocks to ensure that no bruising occurs.

Right: *Once the reassembled chair has been re-upholstered (see pp.67–71), it should last for years before needing further repair.*

POLISHING AND COLOURING

The term "polishing" is used to describe the overall method of filling the grain and enhancing the figure of any piece of wood using shellac polish. The vast majority of polishing work today is commonly known as French polishing, which involves the use of shellac polish combined with oil – often linseed oil – and applied to the wood with a linen rubber.

Within the history of antique furniture, however, there are two very distinctive methods of finishing: varnishing using oil or spirit varnishes, and French polishing, which was introduced only in the 19th century. Both methods create distinctive appearances, and it is the effects of light, oxidation and time that make these polished and waxed surfaces so sought after by today's collectors.

The principles involved in polishing a new surface or repolishing an old surface remain the same: numerous thin layers are built up to form a combined surface. When completed, the polish should have a translucent quality that allows the colour and figure of the wood beneath to be seen. On occasion it may be necessary to tint the polish in order to adjust the final colour. This method of colouring is different from staining with spirit, water or oil, which is the process by which the actual wood tone is changed rather than simply colouring or tinting the polish.

When removing polish from a piece of furniture, it must be done a layer at a time to minimize any damage to the colour and surface of the piece. When the damaged areas have been carefully lifted, further polish can again be applied, a layer at a time, until the required surface appearance is obtained. If too much polish is applied the surface will have a treacle-like appearance; if too little polish is used the grain in the wood will look open and "hungry", resulting in a blotchy effect once the surface has been waxed.

French polishing

Prior to the early 19th century the methods of finishing furniture were mainly the application of varnishes or oils such as linseed and various wax compounds. These were usually applied, often by brush or cloth (cotton rag), after the grain had been sealed with ground brick dust or pumice powder. They served to protect the wood and could be burnished to a soft lustre finish.

In 1820 a new practice, imported from France, came to favour. It was the use of shellac, which comes from the shells of the lac beetle. The shellac, which was dissolved in spirit, was applied layer by layer, giving a hard, glossy finish. Over the years, and with the application of wax, the hard, glossy surfaces mellow, and depending on the style and period of the piece, the surface finish can range from hard and glossy to a soft, almost matt appearance.

Left: *This Regency table has become severely damaged on its polished surface and must be repolished.*

MATERIALS AND EQUIPMENT
- wadding (batting)
- linen
- polish
- fine wire (steel) wool
- methylated spirits (methyl alcohol)
- soft cloth (cotton rag)
- shellac
- linseed oil
- clear beeswax

MAKING AND CHARGING A RUBBER

A rubber is an essential tool for applying a French polish finish and is easy to make. All you need is some wadding (batting) or plain unmedicated cotton wool and a square of linen or similar lint-free cloth. The rubber acts in the same manner as a sponge, absorbing a quantity of the polish (known as charging), which is squeezed out on to the surface being polished when you apply pressure to it. A rubber can also be used to apply a stain to wood.

▷ **1** Lay a 15cm/6in long piece of wadding (batting) on the centre of a piece of linen the size of a large handkerchief.

2 Fold the ends of the linen inward and grasp them in the centre of your palm.

3 With all the outer edges gathered together, twist the ends of the linen to form a tail.

4 The rubber is complete when the tail is completely twisted. For a smaller, more intricate, polishing job, make a smaller rubber to suit.

◁ **5** To charge the rubber, open out the linen to expose the wadding, then pour a small amount of polish on to the wadding. With practice, you will be able to judge the correct quantity. Note that if the rubber is too dry it will not run smoothly over the surface; if it is too wet it will simply lay the polish on the surface.

▷ **6** Refold the linen around the wadding. Squeeze the tail to apply pressure to the wadding, to force the polish through the linen. The more you tighten the tail, the more polish will emerge. After polishing, you can store the rubber for another day.

▷

APPLYING THE POLISH

If the damage to a surface is extensive, it will have to be stripped back with methylated spirits (methyl alcohol) before repolishing, as shown here. New wood is polished in much the same way, except that the grain is first filled with pumice and polish, then sanded flat with very fine or broken down sandpaper.

Once the rubber has been charged, the polish can be applied. This process takes time, and the finish must be left overnight for the polish to harden before it can be buffed to a high sheen or cut back to produce a matt finish.

1 Remove the old polish and wax surface with fine wire (steel) wool and methylated spirits (methyl alcohol).

2 Once the old polish and wax have been removed, wash off the surface with a soft cloth (cotton rag) and methylated spirits.

Tip

When polishing with a rubber (step 3) the idea is to "body up" or fill the grain. This is done by first applying the polish in straight continuous strokes along the grain (below top). The polish is then applied in circular motions (below centre) and finally with wider figure of eight movements (below bottom).

3 Polish the surface using a rubber and shellac (see Tip). Linseed oil can be dripped on to the surface to help lubricate the rubber. This technique, known as "bodying up", fills the grain. Leave for at least 24 hours to harden.

4 When the polish has hardened, cut it back lightly using fine wire wool and working in the direction of the grain. Use light strokes to remove any raised nibs of polish. This also produces a higher gloss finish.

5 Finally, apply a coat of wax. Use light strokes as the polished surface will still be delicate. Allow to stand for a week before use to allow the polish to fully harden.

Right: *When polished, the scratches become invisible and the table has an even, soft sheen that should last for years.*

Waxing

All antique furniture will require waxing during its lifetime. Waxing feeds, protects and nourishes the wood. It is the combination of waxes with natural grease and oxidation that forms the surface patination that is so desirable. Over the generations, various types of wax have been used, with workshops producing their own secret recipes.

One of the most common misconceptions is that the more frequently a piece is waxed. the fuller the finish will be. Over-waxing will result in smeary surfaces, since wax softens wax.

The only remedy for this is to remove all the wax and begin afresh. It is far better to wax at sensible intervals and apply only a very thin layer. Use only natural wax-based products.

MATERIALS AND EQUIPMENT	
• clear wax	• soft cloths (cotton rags)
• soft brush	• brush

WAXING A FLAT SURFACE

1 Apply a thin layer of wax using a soft cloth (cotton rag) impregnated with the chosen wax. Never apply too thick a layer, as this will simply make the rubbing up more difficult and time consuming.

2 Even out the wax using a soft brush. Take care not to mark the surface and make sure you work along the direction of the grain. Use long, steady strokes, working from one side of the surface to the other.

3 Allow the wax to harden for a few minutes, then buff the surface vigorously with a soft cloth, working in the direction of the grain. Finally, use a clean cloth to give the surface a final burnish.

WAXING A CARVED SURFACE

1 Due to the nature of the hollows and relief, it is better to apply a thin coat of wax with a soft brush, making sure that it is neither too hard nor too soft.

2 Allow the wax to harden for a few minutes, then gently burnish the carving with a soft brush. This will remove any surplus wax and even out what remains.

3 Finally, buff the highlights using a soft cloth (cotton rag). Mutton cloth, which is available from most trade suppliers, is ideal for this role.

Staining

Paints and varnishes adhere to the surface of the wood, but stains penetrate it, changing its colour permanently. For this reason, stains are favoured by the restorer. They can enrich dull-looking wood or change the colour of new wood so that it blends in with the rest of the piece of furniture. This bureau has had a new piece of wood added to it that must be stained and polished so that it matches the rest of the piece.

MATERIALS AND EQUIPMENT

- spirit-based (alcohol-based) stain
- cloth (cotton rag)
- wooden dowel
- fine brush
- rubbers
- polish
- methylated spirits (methyl alcohol)
- soft brush
- wax

Tip

Spirit-based (alcohol-based) stains, thinned with methylated spirits (methyl alcohol), are the best stains to use, because they dry very quickly. However, they are harder to obtain and more difficult to use. This is because they can leave obvious overlap marks. Solvent- and water-based stains are available ready mixed and are easier to apply.

1 Use a spirit-based (alcohol-based) stain mixed to match the colour of the furniture. For a small area like this, wrap a piece of cloth (cotton rag) around one end of a dowel and use this to apply the stain to the new piece of wood. If staining a large area, use a brush to apply the stain. Continue until the colour is even, then leave to dry.

2 Check again that the stain is even. If necessary, add another layer, or draw in the grain with a fine brush (see p.43). When you are satisfied with the colour of the dried stain, charge a rubber with polish and apply a layer to the stain, and also to the rest of the bureau to blend in the stained area (see pp.39–40). Allow the polish to dry.

3 Cut back the polish with a rubber charged with a little methylated spirits (methyl alcohol). The new wood should now be indistinguishable from the old.

4 Use a soft brush to apply a thin coat of wax to the new wood, and the rest of the piece of furniture, to give a soft, even sheen. Leave to dry.

Above: *Now stained and polished, the new wood blends seamlessly with the old.*

Graining

During the late 18th and early 19th centuries, rosewood was imported from India, South America and the West Indies for use in the manufacture of furniture. It was an expensive wood, and so only the finest pieces of furniture were made from solid rosewood; other pieces were made from beech, which was a hard-grained, easily workable, cheap native wood. The beech was "grained" with a paint finish to give the appearance of rosewood. Over time, the areas of graining wear away, revealing the beech underneath, as has happened with this Regency chair. In this case, it is necessary to simulate the rosewood graining while also giving it a patinated, antique look. The techniques for distressing are varied and include using smooth stones, fine wire (steel) wool and homemade tools. These should be practised and perfected before use.

MATERIALS AND EQUIPMENT
- light brown spirit-based (alcohol-based) stain
- fine brushes
- screwdriver
- rubber
- polish
- dark brown spirit-based stain
- wax
- cloth (cotton rag)

Above: *An area of the graining has worn away on the chair leg to reveal the beech wood underneath.*

1 Apply a base coat of a light brown stain mixed to match the base colour of the rest of the chair (see p.42). Leave to dry. Charge a rubber with polish and apply a thin layer.

2 Apply a dark brown stain mixed to match the grain of the simulated rosewood, using a fine brush to replicate the pattern. If no residue of graining is left, use a piece of patinated rosewood veneer as a pattern.

3 When the graining is dry, distress the graining effect using a screwdriver, if necessary, to match the original. Give it another rubber of polish to seal in the effect, then wax the chair using a cloth.

Above: *The grained beech chair, on the right of the picture, now looks very similar to the solid rosewood chair on the left. Both these chairs are dining chairs, made c.1810.*

REPAIRING ARMS AND LEGS

The arms and legs of chairs are particularly vulnerable to damage and suffer all manner of problems. The most common of these is scuffing to the feet, which is inevitable and, in severe cases, can lead to the wearing away of the feet until eventually they must be cut off and replaced.

Chairs are often not treated properly, with users leaning back on them too hard or balancing on the rear two legs, which puts tremendous strain on the structure, leading to failure of the joints or breakages of the frame. Even the worst damage can, however, be put right.

Restoring a scuffed foot

Everyday wear and tear takes its toll on most items of furniture, and chairs in particular. This claw and ball chair is more prone to scuffed feet than most because its feet are quite pronounced. Some of the scratches and dents on this foot are quite severe, but they are part of its history and do not need to be repaired. Sympathetic restoration should improve the condition of the item but care, as always, should be taken not to remove any existing colour and patination. The repairs to the surface should be blended in to match the existing finish.

MATERIALS AND EQUIPMENT	
• fine-grade sandpaper	(alcohol-based) stain
• brush	• rubber
• spirit-based	• polish

1 Place the chair on a workbench and go over the scuffed area with fine-grade sandpaper until you have removed the old polish and any other debris.

2 Mix some stain to the required colour (see p.30) and brush this over the foot, then use a rubber to polish the foot to match the rest of the chair (see pp.39–40).

Above: *The restored foot has not been made to look brand new, which would make it stand out from the rest of the chair, but has simply had its colour and sheen restored.*

Replacing a chewed arm

Some dogs and cats have a propensity for gnawing, chewing or sharpening their teeth on wooden furniture. Sometimes the damage inflicted is just a few scratches, but in other cases the furniture needs substantial rebuilding. This 18th-century Cuban mahogany child's rocking chair has had its arm and leg almost completely chewed off by the family dog. Before the arm and leg can be rebuilt, some of the damaged wood must be removed.

MATERIALS AND EQUIPMENT
- Cuban mahogany
- PVA (white) glue
- sash clamp
- coping saw
- spokeshave
- fine-grade sandpaper
- brush
- spirit-based (alcohol-based) stain
- rubber
- polish

Above: *The chewed-off arm*

1 Select appropriate replacement mahogany pieces and build up the rough shape of the arm in layers, using PVA (white) glue, and starting on the inside surface. Make the rebuilt arm slightly larger than the original.

2 Glue a single block of mahogany to the outer surface, and a larger block to the front of this. Then clamp the rebuilt arm in position. Leave the sash clamp in position until the glue is dry.

3 Remove the clamp and draw the shape of the arm on the new wood, slightly larger than the original. Cut along this line with a coping saw.

4 Shape the surface with a spokeshave, copying the contours of the other arm. Continue until you have an exact match. Repeat this process for the damaged leg.

5 Smooth both repairs with fine-grade sandpaper. Mix some stain to the required colour (see p.30), brush this over the repairs, then polish to match the rest of the chair.

Right: *Once polished, the repairs become invisible, restoring the chair to its former state.*

Repairing a cabriole leg

This 19th-century Victorian walnut balloon-back chair has a typical break to its leg. The curved shape of the cabriole leg, combined with the inherent weakness of walnut along the grain, means that this type of chair design is particularly vulnerable to damage, especially if misused.

Although this leg has a clean break, simply regluing it would not give it enough strength. Instead, a dowel must be inserted into holes drilled in both parts of the leg, which are then glued together to give a strong and lasting repair. The technique is quite straightforward, the most critical stage being the alignment and drilling of the dowel holes in the two broken pieces. Fortunately, there is a simple method of achieving this, using nothing more than a nail.

MATERIALS AND EQUIPMENT
- hammer
- 25mm (1in) nail
- snips or cutters
- pliers
- drill
- wood drill bits
- dowel
- thin chisel
- wood glue
- snap clamps
- fine-grade sandpaper
- rubber
- polish

▷ **1** Place the chair upside down on a protected workbench. Hammer a 25mm/1in nail halfway into the centre of the upper section of the leg to provide a means of marking matching dowel hole positions on both pieces of the leg.

2 Cut the nail to a short, sharp point using a pair of snips or cutters.

3 The projecting piece of nail will now be used to mark the centre of the lower section of the leg.

4 Bring the two sections of the leg together and tap the lower section down so that the nail leaves an indentation on its broken surface. Remove the lower section and pull out the piece of nail with a pair of pliers.

5 Drill a small pilot hole in both sections of the leg, using the indentations left by the nail as guides.

6 Select a dowel that is about a third of the width of the leg and about 75mm/3in long. Use a drill bit of the same size as the dowel to drill holes about 38mm/1½in deep in both sections of the leg.

7 Rest the dowel against a block fixed to the workbench, and use a thin chisel to cut a narrow sliver along the length of the dowel. This will allow excess glue to escape.

◁ **8** Apply glue to both matching faces and the dowel, then insert the dowel into the upper section, tapping it down with a hammer if necessary, and bring the two parts together.

▷ **9** Make sure that the edges are flush, then clamp the leg sections together with snap clamps and leave the glue to dry.

10 Remove the clamps and stand the chair upright. Sandpaper the area of repair, then polish it so that it matches the rest of the chair (see pp.39–40).

Right: *Once polished, the repair should not be visible, while the strength of the chair leg will have been increased significantly.*

Repairing a broken upright

This Georgian chair shows a common problem: the user has sat back perhaps a little too heavily and broken the chair at the weakest point, along the long grain, just above the seat level.

In this instance, a previous repair had been carried out and the break had followed the line of the old damage. This illustrates how make-shift repairs are only temporary measures. To create a more permanent repair, a new piece of wood must be inserted to enable the two parts of the broken upright to be secured properly.

MATERIALS AND EQUIPMENT	
• white cardboard	• sash clamps
• profile gauge	• fine-grade
• tenon saw	sandpaper
• plane	• fine brush
• scissors	• stain
• mahogany	• rubber
• band saw	• polish
• PVA (white) glue	
• G-clamps	
• clamping blocks	
• spokeshave	

1 Place the chair on a protected workbench, remove the upholstery (see pp.34–35), then knock the chair apart following steps 1–5 on pp.35–36. Place the undamaged upright on a large piece of white cardboard and use a profile gauge to trace its outline. This is the template (pattern) for the new piece of wood.

2 Now knock the back uprights apart from the stretcher, back seat rail, back support and back top rail.

Tip

When marking out a template on a shaped upright, a simple workshop-made profile gauge is best. Join an upright to a face plate at right angles and drill a hole through that allows the refill from a ballpoint pen to be inserted.

3 Compare the broken upright to the traced outline.

◁ **5** Cut out the cardboard template. Place it on a matching piece of mahogany, then mark the correct shape. Cut along this line with a band saw.

4 Cut away the damage with a tenon saw and plane the edges of the two parts flat. Lay the parts on the pattern in the correct position. The gap will indicate the size of the new part to be inserted.

6 Glue the matching piece of mahogany securely into position between the two pieces of the upright. Clamp it securely and leave to dry overnight – this will ensure a secure bond.

7 Form the correct shape with a spokeshave, using the undamaged upright as your guide. Cut three new mortises (see p.57) in the upright to house the tenons of the side and back seat rails and the back support.

8 Reassemble the chair back and clamp until dry. Remove the clamps, then finish shaping the new wood with fine-grade sandpaper.

◁ **9** The final shape should now match the other upright exactly. Stain the replacement mahogany (see p.42) and polish the repairs to match the existing chair (see pp.39–40) before reassembling the whole chair (see pp.36–37). Replace the upholstery (see pp.67–71).

Right: *The new joint on the restored chair should be almost invisible.*

Repairing a broken arm

Almost all arms on chairs have two points of fixing: one on a back upright, the other against a seat rail. Some are housed with a tenon or dovetail joint, while others may simply be placed flush and held with large screws. When faced with a damaged arm, as with all other restoration work, the first step is to examine the damage and ascertain the construction methods used in the piece. With this information, the correct procedure and techniques can then be determined.

The arm of this maple chair had become loose against both the seat rail and the back upright. This could have been caused by any number of events, including being dropped or knocked, or being picked up by the arms rather than by the seat. The arm must be removed and assessed before being reassembled.

MATERIALS AND EQUIPMENT

- screwdriver
- hammer
- hardwood block
- chisel
- toothbrush
- PVA (white) glue
- G-clamp
- snap clamps
- clamping blocks

1 Place the chair on its side on a workbench, and loosen and remove the two large screws that hold the arm support to the side seat rail. The screws, which are fixed from the inside of the rail, are usually hidden by the drop-in upholstered seat. Keep the screws for reattaching the arm support.

2 Gently ease the arm tenon out of the mortise in the back upright, so that the whole arm structure is now detached from the chair. The dowel peg joint between the arm and arm support is also found to be loose. Place the arm on the workbench and tap off the joint using a block of hardwood and a hammer.

3 Remove any lumps of old glue from the joints using a sharp chisel, taking care not to mark any polished areas. If a crystalline residue is present, then an animal adhesive has been used; remove this with an old toothbrush and hot water. The water will soften and dissolve the glue, but make sure that it does not run and cause marks.

Left: *Once the glue has dried and the clamps have been removed, the chair should be as sturdy as when first made.*

4 Check that all the joints are tight, then reglue them and reattach the arm and the support to each other and to the chair. Use a G-clamp to secure the support to the seat rail and snap clamps to secure the arm to the back upright and the arm to the arm support. Use clamping blocks at all clamping points; if the chair upright is bowed, you will need to pre-shape a clamping block to fit.

Removing a broken screw

If a screw has remained in a piece of furniture for many years, perhaps even hundreds of years, it may have become weak, and when you try to remove it, the shank may break. If this happens, there are three possible solutions.

You may be able to make a new, temporary screw from the damaged one by cutting a new slot in the broken shank (see steps).

Alternatively, you could drill a hole, slightly larger than the screw shank, down the side of the screw, then tap it sideways into this hole with a screwdriver. This will allow you to remove it with a pair of long-nose (needlenose) pliers. You will have to plug the hole with a glued-in wooden dowel before reusing it.

Finally, you could simply drill out the screw with a metal drill bit of the same size, or slightly larger; but again you will have to plug the resulting hole in order to be able to reuse it.

1 *If the shank of a screw breaks when you try to remove it, leaving a stub proud of the surface, cut a new slot in the end of the shank with a hacksaw.*

2 *Remove the screw simply by undoing it in the normal fashion. The metal will be weak, so use a screwdriver that fits snugly into the slot.*

51

Reeding a turned chair leg

During the 18th century, reeded decoration on turned legs came into fashion. The legs were tapered, and so the reeding also had to taper from top to bottom, as well as being equally balanced around the leg. In order to do this work, a scratch box is used (see below). The scratch box has parallel sides and adjustable centre points at each end to allow a shaped reed cutter to be applied to the turned leg. In this instance, one leg from a Sheraton chair, c.1790, has been broken and lost, so a replacement is needed.

Above: *A scratch box*

MATERIALS AND EQUIPMENT
- callipers
- wood
- lathe
- turning tools
- dividers
- band saw or scraper
- rat-tail file
- scratch box
- try square (combination square)
- back bent chisel
- cabinet scraper
- fine-grade sandpaper
- gouge
- fine brush
- stain
- rubber
- polish
- wax

◁ **1** Take the measurements for the template (pattern) leg from the original leg, using callipers for the circumference. Make sure that enough wood is left to allow for the reeds to be scratched. Turn the template leg on the lathe.

◁ **2** Using a pair of dividers, measure the width of the reed. When set, transfer the dividers to the template leg and mark divisions at the top of the leg corresponding to the original.

3 Now cut the reed cutter to the correct size and profile using an old band saw or scraper. As the blade will scrape and edge rather than cut it, make sure the edge is at a 90-degree angle to the side.

◁ **4** Fit the leg to the scratch box just below the height of the sides. To ensure that it is set parallel, measure the distance from the height of the sides both at the top and bottom of the leg with a try square (combination square).

▷ **5** Pass the cutter back and forth to scratch the reed into the leg. This should be done with an even pressure. When the reed is scratched, revolve the leg to the next division mark and scratch the next reed.

6 The scratch blade in the cutter will scratch a V shape. However, you can round it using a back bent chisel if you want a more rounded shape.

7 Use a cabinet scraper to clean the reed again. This will give a clean finish, as it is the same shape as the actual reeds. Then use fine-grade sandpaper with an overloe.

8 On certain reeded legs the top is not square but rounded. If you want to create this effect, use a gouge.

◁ **9** When finished, compare the new leg against the original to ensure that they are a good match. Note that enough wood is left at the top to allow a new mortise to be cut and joined to the seat rails.

Right: *The new leg can now be stained, polished and waxed (see pp.39–42), and any necessary distressing may be applied to make it match the patina of the other legs.*

REPAIRING BACKS AND FRAMES

The most common fault found in chair frames is joint damage, such as broken mortise and tenon or dowel joints. Top rails are liable to break at the weak short grain at the end of each rail. Repairs can necessitate fairly major surgery on the broken parts, but the results can be very effective. Dowel joints are easiest to fix, since the broken dowels can simply be drilled out and replaced with new ones. Broken tenons, however, are more difficult, as their strength comes originally from being an integral part of the piece being joined. The answer is to replace the broken piece by gluing a wooden tongue into a slot cut in the frame piece.

Cutting in a tenon joint

The protruding piece of wood on a side seat rail is a tenon; the recess it slots into in a back upright is a mortise. This is the standard joint found on frame chairs, but on occasion the tenon can break. The tenon on this mahogany Regency chair has snapped off completely and been lost.

To make a repair, a new piece of wood must be cut to size and glued into a slot cut into the seat rail, before being shaped to fit snugly within the mortise. The mortise itself does not need repairing. When sanded and polished, the repair will not be noticeable.

MATERIALS AND EQUIPMENT
- mortise gauge
- tenon saw
- mortise chisel
- heavy mallet
- mahogany
- PVA (white) glue
- clamping blocks
- G-clamp
- square rule
- spokeshave
- bench hook
- block plane
- fine brush
- stain

1 Knock the chair apart following steps 1–5 on pp.35–36. Set a mortise gauge to the width of the mortise in the upright, then run it over the broken end of the side seat rail and 10cm/4in down its underside.

2 Place the damaged side seat rail in a vice. Cut along the lines made by the mortise gauge with a tenon saw. It is important not to cut beyond the marks made by the mortise gauge.

3 Remove the mahogany from between the cut lines with a mortise chisel and a heavy mallet. It is important to cut to a reasonable depth in the rail to ensure that the new joint will be sufficiently strong.

4 Cut a piece of mahogany to fit in the new slot in the side seat rail, allowing about 15cm/6in to protrude.

5 Apply PVA (white) glue to the new wood and insert it into the side seat rail. Clamp the side seat rail between two clamping blocks and leave to dry.

6 Remove the clamp and blocks. Place a square rule against the cut end of the side seat rail and draw a pencil line to mark out the upper end of the tenon. Repeat for the lower end and the top, which should match the depth of the mortise.

7 Cut along the pencil lines with a tenon saw, then use a spokeshave to remove the excess wood from the bottom of the rail.

8 Place the side seat rail on a bench hook (see Tip below) and use a block plane to make the tenon the correct width. Check the fit of the tenon in the mortise repeatedly during this procedure to ensure a tight fit.

9 Once the tenon has been planed to fit exactly in the mortise, reassemble the chair (see pp.36–37) and leave to dry.

Right: *When the glue has dried, the clamps can be removed, and the underside of the tenon in the side seat rail stained to match the rest of the chair (see p.42). The new joint should last for many more years.*

Tip

A bench hook comprises a board with a batten at each end, one of which butts against the edge of the bench top, while the other provides a stop for the workpiece to hold it securely. To make one, use a piece of 2.5cm/1in thick board, about 25cm/10in long and 17.5cm/7in wide. Cut two lengths of batten about 2.5cm/1in square and 12.5cm/5in long. Glue one of these flush with one end and the left-hand edge of the board. Turn the board over and glue the remaining batten to the other end, again flush with the left-hand edge.

Replacing a mortise and tenon joint

The mortise and tenon on this George III mahogany chair frame have both been damaged. An earlier repair was badly executed, so a new mortise and tenon will have to be cut and fitted. This involves cutting away the damaged wood, splicing in new pieces of similar material and forming the two halves of the joint. The result will be as strong as the original joint.

MATERIALS AND EQUIPMENT
- tenon saw
- mahogany
- PVA (white) glue
- G-clamp
- spokeshave
- try square (combination square)
- utility knife
- medium- and fine-grade sandpaper
- paring chisel
- drill
- wood drill bit
- mortise chisel
- carving tools
- mortise gauge

1 Knock the chair apart following steps 1–6 on pp.35–36, and place the side seat rail in a vice. Cut away the existing repair wood with a tenon saw to leave a flat surface for the new wood to adhere to.

2 Cut a piece of mahogany for a replacement tenon. Apply PVA (white) glue and attach the new piece to the seat rail. Clamp until dry, then shape the wood to follow the rail's curve with a spokeshave.

3 Using the undamaged side seat rail as a guide, transfer the measurements of the tenon on to the new wood with a try square (combination square) and utility knife. Cut the tenon.

◁ **4** Smooth the new wood, including the newly cut tenon joint, with sandpaper.

5 Cut out the damaged wood and the old repair from the leg with a paring chisel, leaving a wedge-shaped cut-out. Shape a piece of new wood to fit this and glue it in place. Clamp until dry, then remove the clamp.

6 Remove the remains of the side seat rail tenon, which is lodged in the mortise joint, by first drilling access holes, then using a mortise chisel to clean out the remaining wood.

7 Place the leg in a vice and cut the new wood to size. Use carving tools to shape it to match the rest of the leg. Finish by sanding it smooth with medium-grade sandpaper.

8 You now need to cut a new mortise into the new wood. Use a mortise gauge to mark the correct width of the mortise and then a mortise chisel to remove the wood.

◁ **9** Smooth the joint with fine-grade sandpaper, then check that the tenon fits snugly into the mortise. Make any necessary final adjustments using sandpaper to ensure a perfect fit.

Above: *The restored mortise and tenon joint will have the strength of the original. The chair can now be reassembled.*

Dowel joint repair

While the most common type of joint used in furniture construction during the 17th, 18th and 19th centuries was the mortise and tenon, by the mid-19th century, due to the increase of furniture production and the need for less time-consuming construction techniques, the dowel joint was being used in certain furniture manufacture. Although similar to the mortise and tenon joint in purpose, the dowel joint employs inset dowels to connect two pieces together. Like the mortise and tenon, however, it does, on occasion, break and have to be replaced.

The dowel joints of this mid-19th-century Victorian balloon-back chair had broken. An earlier repair between the frame and back upright, utilizing a metal bracket, was not successful, and the joint needed to be repaired properly. Once the upholstery had been removed and the chair knocked apart (steps 1–5 on pp.35–36), the extent of the damage could be ascertained. The dowels in one joint had broken off and needed removing from the back upright, while the dowels in the other joint had been removed and covered with a mahogany patch; new holes would need to be drilled into this patch.

MATERIALS AND EQUIPMENT
- drill
- wood drill bits
- tenon saw
- dowels
- PVA (white) glue
- hammer
- panel pins (brads)
- pincers
- sash clamps
- clamping blocks
- masking tape
- hand drill
- chisel
- rubber
- polish

◁ **1** Place the left-hand upright in a vice and drill out the remaining dowel pieces. The auger bit used must be the same diameter as the dowels. Also drill out the remaining dowel pieces in the corresponding side seat rail, then cut and glue new lengths of dowel into these seat rail holes.

▷ **2** Turning now to the problem of the patched upright, place the other side seat rail in a vice. Fit a length of dowel into each of the two seat rail dowel joint holes. Do not glue them in, but cut them flush with the shoulder of the joint.

3 Hammer a panel pin (brad) into the centre of each of the dowel pieces (known as location pegs), and cut back the ends with pincers to leave sharp points standing proud of the surface.

4 Position the seat rail correctly against the back upright and use a sash clamp to pull it into place. Clamp the other side seat rail to keep the frame square. Hold the clamping blocks in place with masking tape.

5 Release the clamps and remove the front and side seat rail structure. The location pins will have marked the correct positions of the new dowel holes in the mahogany patch.

6 Hand drill pilot holes into the pin marks, opening them up to the size of the dowels with an auger bit. Drill at an angle that is square to the back seat rail, so the shoulder of the joint pulls up flush with the upright.

7 Remove the location pegs by gripping the pins and pulling them out. Use the location pegs to determine the correct length of the new dowels required.

8 Cut and glue the new dowels into the joint, then cut channels into the dowels with a chisel. These grooves allow any excess glue to escape from the joint. Reassemble the chair (see pp.36–37).

Right: *After the glue has dried and the clamps have been removed, give the chair a rubber of polish (see pp.39–40). At this stage, it is ready to be re-upholstered (see pp.67–71). The joint is now as strong as it was when the chair was first constructed.*

Repairing a broken back

A common problem with chairs is that they can break along their top rails. This can be caused by a diner leaning back too hard or a chair being knocked over and the joints shattering. Many breakages of this type require extensive repair work.

In this instance, the top rail of a George III Cuban mahogany dining chair has become broken, and, unfortunately, one of the tenons was smashed beyond repair. An added complication was the fact that the chair retained its original horsehair upholstery, and it was considered wisest to leave the seat *in situ* during restoration. This meant that extra care had to be taken when making the repair.

MATERIALS AND EQUIPMENT

- masking tape
- tenon saw
- Cuban mahogany
- coping saw
- PVA (white) glue
- G-clamp
- clamping block
- mortise gauge
- chisels
- hammer
- nails
- spokeshave
- band clamps
- fine-grade sandpaper
- flat-bladed knife
- stopping wax
- brush
- stain
- rubber
- polish

▷ **1** Remove the top rail and vertical back supports, which will all be joined by mortise and tenon joints. In this instance, the top rail split into three parts on removal. Label the different parts with masking tape (see p.35).

◁ **3** Having removed the damaged section from the right-hand upright, select a suitable piece of matching Cuban mahogany. Holding it in position, draw the outline of the back upright on it. Cut along this line with a coping saw.

2 A new tenon must be cut to replace the smashed one, but first a section of mahogany must be let into the back upright. Line the vice with old baize and cut out the damaged section with a tenon saw.

◁ **4** Glue the mahogany insert into place. Clamp it into position with a G-clamp and clamping blocks and allow the glue to set. This insert will form the new tenon joint.

◁ **5** Measure the tenon on the opposite side upright with a mortise gauge. Transcribe this dimension to the new wood.

6 Cut the new tenon with a tenon saw. Make it slightly wider than the scored lines so that you can pare it down later to produce a really tight and accurate fit.

◁ **7** Clean up the joint using a sharp paring chisel. Check the measurement repeatedly against the top rail mortise to ensure a tight fit.

8 The mortise on the left-hand side of the top rail has broken away. Glue back any large sections, pinning the joints together with nails for extra strength. Countersink the heads of the nails.

9 Replace the badly smashed piece from the top rail with sections of Cuban mahogany, trimming it roughly to shape with a chisel.

▷

61

Repairing a broken back...continued

10 Continue shaping the new piece of wood on the top rail with a spokeshave, but do not shape the insert at the joint until the chair has been reassembled. This will allow it to be blended into the upright.

11 Reglue the vertical supports to the top rail and the back seat rail, then reglue the back uprights and top rail together. Note that the rail insert (right) has not yet been shaped.

◁ **12** Use nylon band clamps to apply pressure. These are made from nylon straps fitted with ratchets that allow an even pressure to be applied. Band clamps are ideal for gluing shaped chair backs. When the glue has dried, remove the clamps and shape the mahogany inserts to follow the line of the back upright and the top rail. Finish the repair by smoothing it with fine-grade sandpaper. Using a flat-bladed knife, fill the countersunk nail holes (see step 8) with stopping wax.

Right: *Stain (see p.42) and polish (see pp.39–40) the repairs to match the existing surface. By remaking the smashed parts of the joints, rather than simply gluing them back together, you will have restored the strength of the chair completely.*

Repairing a top rail

The top rail of this 19th-century Regency mahogany chair has become loose due to a break in the stopped dovetail joint. It is old damage, and at some point a temporary repair had been made using a dowel to strengthen the joint, but this did not stop it breaking a second time.

The joint now needs to be repaired properly. The process will involve splicing out the damaged areas from the upright and the top rail and remaking both parts of the joint.

MATERIALS AND EQUIPMENT
- tenon saw
- Cuban mahogany
- plane
- PVA (white) glue
- G-clamp
- spokeshaves
- fine-grade sandpaper
- chisel
- sash clamp

1 First remove the damaged area of the upright using a tenon saw. Cut away an angled splice to ensure that the new joint will be strong and less noticeable.

2 Cut a suitable piece of Cuban mahogany roughly to size with a tenon saw. Plane one side flush and glue to the upright. Apply G-clamps overnight. When the joint is tight, roughly shape the new wood using a spokeshave.

3 Using a finer spokeshave, shape the new wood, carefully copying the profile of the intact upright. The repair should blend seamlessly with the original. Finish with fine sandpaper.

4 To repair the top rail, remove the damaged areas of wood with a sharp chisel. To make a good joint, ensure that the edges are clean and crisp.

5 Glue together the upright and top rail using PVA (white) glue. Apply sash clamps overnight to ensure a strong joint.

Above: *When the joint is tight, the new wood is stained to match the original wood and then polished. The restored area should be almost invisible.*

UPHOLSTERY

The majority of antique seating furniture, ranging from stools to settees, will need to be upholstered in one form or another. The choice of fabric used will be a personal one, but you should always endeavour to match the style and method of upholstery to the relevant period, since the construction of the chair, stool or settee will reflect the original cabinet-maker's choice of upholstering. To alter this will not only spoil the aesthetics of the whole piece but can also devalue the chair. Also, for authenticity, use tacks rather than staples when reupholstering.

The earliest recorded mention of upholstery was during the 15th century. However, during this period it was the beds and state canopies that received lavish fabric treatments, with seating being confined in the main to squab or loose cushions. These chairs would have been filled with down or horsehair, but by the 16th century the X-frame chair was in use, often covered with velvet or silk damask (see p.8).

Upholstery rapidly became more fashionable, and by the 18th century there were numerous types and styles of upholstery, ranging from the simple squab seat, to be used with a cane seat, to elaborate wing chairs, which were fully upholstered with only their show-wood legs showing.

The techniques and materials used can alter depending on the origin of the chair, but although modern materials are now available, traditional ones should be favoured whenever possible.

Left: *A Regency dining chair with a squab seat to protect the canework seat underneath.*

Right: *A George III dining chair with a drop-in seat.*

Right: *A George II dining chair with a stuff-over seat and close nail decoration.*

Above: *An elegant Queen Anne wing chair with fully upholstered back and arms and a down-filled loose cushion.*

Left: *A Regency bergère chair with deep-buttoned leather squab seat.*

Caning

Cane seating can be found in various patterns and styles, although the most common design found on antique furniture is the traditional six-way pattern shown here. Cane is actually rattan, which grows in tropical areas of the Far East, and to obtain the cane, strips are cut from the outside of the rattan, then reduced to various widths, which are classified on a scale of 0 to 6. This outer part of the rattan is used for seating, while the inner parts are employed for basketwork. The tools required are few, and it is very much a technique that requires patience and care. The most common examples of canework are chairs, stools and bed heads.

The method used in chairs is known as open caning, which describes the technique of interweaving long lengths of cane to form a strong, flexible platform on which a squab seat is usually placed. Prior to beginning work, remove all the old cane, including the pegs. The best method of doing this is to drill them out with a drill bit that is slightly smaller in diameter than the holes. Also make sure that the seat frame is tight, since caning a loose or rickety chair is pointless.

Tip

Although the cane can be worked dry, the task will be easier if it is soaked in water for a minute or two first and kept wrapped in a damp cloth to mellow while the seat is being worked. Do not make it too wet or keep it damp for too long, because either of these conditions will cause the cane to deteriorate.

MATERIALS AND EQUIPMENT
- cane
- cloths (cotton rags)
- rattan pegs
- shell bodkin
- secateurs (pruners)
- hammer
- stain or wax

1 The first stage, or first setting as it is known, is to thread damp cane (see Tip) through the holes from side to side. Hold the cane in place with a rattan peg, then pull the cane across the frame and thread it down through the opposite hole. After securing it with a temporary peg, thread the cane up through the adjacent hole from the underside and repeat the process.

2 Change direction and lay cane at right angles to the first setting, i.e. from front to back. This is the first weaving. Now thread a second row of cane through the same holes as the first setting, but slightly to the right to form a double-width band. This is the second setting.

▷

Caning...continued

3 The second weaving, which involves laying a second strand of cane from front to back, differs from the first weaving in that this strand is woven over the second setting and under the first setting, which interlocks all four cane bands. Use a shell bodkin to help thread the cane through the various stages of weaving.

4 For the first diagonal weave, or first crossing as it is known, you need to thread cane over the settings and under the weavings, i.e. over the double cane bands set from side to side, and under those woven from front to back.

5 Repeat the process across the other diagonal. This second crossing involves weaving the cane under the settings and over the weavings. This is the opposite to the first crossing. The cane should slip neatly into the corners between the first weaving and the second setting.

6 Hold the cane securely in place by inserting rattan pegs in the holes, cutting them flush with a pair of garden secateurs (pruners). No glue is used, you just hammer the pegs home with a gentle tap.

Above: *When completed, the seat should exhibit an evenly woven geometric pattern that will give strength and flexibility. You can leave the cane in its natural state, but it is often better to apply some stained wax or a water-based stain (see pp.41 and 42).*

Beaded finish

Prior to 1850 a pegged finish (as shown above) was generally used. After this date a decorative beaded finish was favoured (see right). Always select the finish that fits with the period of the chair you are restoring.

Upholstering a stuff-over seat

There are several ways to upholster a chair. The style and method employed will be dictated by the period and design of the chair, but the most common method in most 18th- and 19th-century furniture is that of over webbing. If carried out correctly, the chair will have an even, flat line that will be comfortable and durable and, most importantly, will show off the lines of the chair to their best effect.

Today, the staple gun is often used alongside the traditional tack and hammer in the upholstery workshop, but while the staple gun undoubtedly saves time, the tack and hammer are always the choice of the quality restoration workshop.

This chair will be upholstered using traditional methods and tools. Although you may already possess some of the tools – such as the mallet, pincers and scissors – the more unusual items will need seeking out from specialist tool suppliers and stores that stock furnishing materials. Alternatively, look out for traditional examples in car boot sales and second-hand shops.

MATERIALS AND EQUIPMENT
- webbing
- tacks
- hammer
- web stretcher
- mallet
- pincers
- scissors
- hessian (burlap)
- twine
- upholstery
- needles
- horsehair
- calico
- upholstery pins
- skin wadding (batting)
- top fabric
- gimp pins
- braid finish
- superglue
- tack hammer

1 Fold over the ends of four lengths of webbing and tack them to the back of the chair frame at equal intervals. Stretch the webbing across to the front of the frame using a web stretcher, fold over the ends and tack them down. Repeat across the sides of the frame, interweaving the lengths of webbing as shown.

2 Cut a piece of hessian (burlap) slightly larger than the seat frame. Place it on top of the webbing, fold the edges over and tack it down to secure.

3 Stitch several lines of large, looping stitches around the edge of the hessian and across the centre using an upholstery needle. These loops will be used to keep the horsehair in place.

4 Starting from the middle of the seat and working outward, place handfuls of horsehair on the hessian and tease it under the twine loops to secure. Continue until the horsehair sits evenly. ▷

Upholstering a stuff-over seat...continued

◁ **5** Cut a second piece of hessian and drape it over the horsehair. Secure the hessian with temporary tacks along the chair frame. Stitch further twine loops through the seat with a long needle; these are used to pull the seating flat as well as to hold the horsehair in place.

▷ **6** Remove the temporary tacks with a mallet and tack lifter. Trim the hessian to size, then tack all the way around the seat, taking particular care at the corners. Mistakes at this stage will be very difficult to rectify later.

7 Stitch more ties through the seat, then use the long needle to apply a blind stitch just above the tack line, and also on the top edge, about 2.5cm/1in above the tack line. This begins the process of making the finished edge and will hold the horsehair in place for the next stage.

8 Use the ties to readjust the stuffing, flattening it as much as possible, then blind stitch around the top edges once more, just outside the existing stitches, paying special attention to the corners. When completed, the seat should be flat with the edges held firmly in place.

9 Place another layer of horsehair on the hessian and tease it to fit the dimensions of the seat exactly, producing a slightly domed shape.

◁ **10** Cover the horsehair with a piece of calico. Pull the calico tight and secure it with upholstery pins. The seat should be smooth and regular in shape.

▷**11** Fold in the corners of the calico and cut to fit. Tack the calico in position and remove the upholstery pins.

12 Cut a piece of skin wadding (batting) to double the length of the seat, fold it in two and place it on the seat. This will prevent the coarse horsehair from coming through.

13 Lay the top cover on the wadding. Fit temporary tacks to the underside of the seat rails so that you can check that any pattern is aligned and the fabric is not overstretched.

14 Adjust the temporary tacks as necessary. Secure the fabric by hammering more tacks into the underside of the seat rails. Trim the corners and fold them away, making sure the folds are on the outside edge.

Left: *The newly upholstered seat should enhance the overall design of the chair, be comfortable to sit on and, most importantly, last for many years.*

15 Use small gimp pins hammered in with a tack hammer to hold in the corners, if necessary. The top cover should look smooth and even.

16 Apply the braid finish with superglue and snip off any loose threads.

Finishes

There are several ways of finishing the upholstery of a chair. These include applying attractive finishing techniques to the seat itself and adding various types of decorative edging around the seat rail. The latter have a practical purpose, too, since they are used to provide a neat finish to the edges of the top fabric.

SPACE NAILING

This technique involves applying a braid with superglue, then hammering in large-headed nails at regular intervals. It is suitable for late 18th-century and Regency styles.

CLOSE NAILING

This technique, as the name suggests, involves forming a border of closely spaced nails tacked into the seat rail. It is suitable for tapestry fabrics and a mid-18th-century look.

BRAID

There are numerous braids to choose from, in all colours, tones and styles. They are usually applied with superglue and can be employed with any suitable fabric.

ROPE AND PIPING

Rope and piping finishes are used to emphasize the edges of cushions and seats. When used on upholstered seats they are known as "self piping" and give a sculptured look to a seat.

Floating buttons

The use of five floating buttons, combined with space nailing on a braid border, gives a smart, stylish finish. The technique of fitting the buttons is shown below.

1 *Pass some upholstery thread through a button, then use a long needle to pass the double threads down through the seat.*

2 *Guide the button into position while pulling the threads taut underneath. The button should form a gentle dip in the seat.*

3 *Tie off the threads from the underside of the seat, using a scrap (offcut) of webbing to spread the pressure. Repeat for the other four buttons.*

PROJECT: RAYNHAM CHAIR

The age of this chair was unknown when it was bought from an auction house. The material, Cuban mahogany, the style of the internal seat rails and the carving indicated that it was a mid-18th-century piece and almost identical to a number attributed to Thomas Chippendale or William Vile for the Marquess of Townsend at Raynham Hall, Norfolk. As such, it could be an important piece and

would require sympathetic restoration to bring it back to its original condition. It needed a considerable amount of work to the frame to overcome the ravages of time, including the replacement of parts that were missing with new Cuban mahogany. However, with a great deal of patience and careful work, it was possible to re-create the beauty of the original craftsmanship.

ASSESSING THE PROJECT

This chair was in need of comprehensive restoration. On removing the upholstery (which revealed original hay stuffing), it became clear that the seat frame was worm-eaten and loose, and new wood would be needed to strengthen it. Furthermore, the legs appeared to be too short for the height of the chair, and they were missing areas of carving. The feet looked as though they had been cut down and they did not have castors.

The seat frame
• loose
• worm-eaten wood

The feet
• wrong shape
• castors missing

The legs
• incorrect height
• areas of carving
  missing

Repairing the seat frame

The seat frame was found to be loose and, in areas, the rails were extensively damaged by woodworm. As with all restoration projects, it is important to keep as much of the original material as possible, so the seat frame must be knocked apart carefully and then restored sympathetically. The method used is to remove the core from the original wood and fill the space with a core of new wood. In this way, the strength of the chair can be restored with the new strong core, while the retained exterior of original wood helps to confirm the age of the piece. Chairs that have been completely rerailed can be substantially devalued.

Above right: *Woodworm damage*

MATERIALS AND EQUIPMENT
- tack lifter
- hammer
- hardwood block
- masking tape
- circular saw

- beech
- PVA (white) glue
- clamping blocks
- G-clamps

- tenon saw
- fine brush
- spirit-based (alcohol-based) stain

1 Remove the upholstery and set it aside (see pp.34–35). Note that the chair still has hay as part of its stuffing, indicating that it was last fully re-upholstered in the 19th century. With the upholstery removed, it could be seen that the seat rails were original throughout.

2 Use a tack lifter to free the ends of the now-revealed webbing and strip it away. The springs, which are stitched to the webbing, can be seen beneath the webbing.

3 Knock the chair apart completely (see pp.35–36) using a hammer and a hardwood block. The block ensures that an even pressure is applied and that no damage is caused to the mahogany surface.

▷

Repairing the seat frame...continued

◁ **4** Label the individual parts as you remove them. Although it would be difficult to confuse the pieces with just one chair, this could easily happen if there were more than one, so it is good workshop practice to label everything.

5 One of the seat rails has been radically attacked by woodworm and must have a new core inserted. Cut through the length of the seat rail using a circular saw, removing the inner core. Note that for the sake of clearer photography the safety guard has been removed.

▷ **6** Cut a central core from a piece of beech to the same dimensions as the one removed. The original face wood from the rail, which is quite damaged, will serve little more than a cosmetic role, so the beech insert, which will provide the strength, should be a good piece of wood, free from any knots or faults.

7 Glue the three lengths of wood together, with the beech (which will form the tenon) in the middle. Position some newspaper (to protect against leaking glue) and some clamping blocks, then clamp the three parts together and leave to dry. Cut a tenon joint (see p.55).

◁ **8** Although the other seat rails do not need new cores, they do have worm-damaged areas that need to be patched with new beech. It is important, however, to retain as much of the original seat rails as possible. Make sure that any joints that need to be restored still fit prior to the chair being reglued. Continue until all the seat frame damage is repaired, then stain the repairs to match the original wood.

Repairing the feet

Now that the seat frame has been repaired, attention can be given to the problem of the shortened legs. At some stage in their history, their length has been reduced by about 4cm/1½in, almost certainly because of damage. This gives the chair an unbalanced appearance. The answer is to glue mahogany blocks to the legs and to shape them to fit in with the overall design. Damaged areas of moulding around the bottom of the old legs are replaced with new wood, which is then carved and shaped to match the undamaged areas.

MATERIALS AND EQUIPMENT
- tenon saw
- Cuban mahogany
- PVA (white) glue
- sash clamps
- clamping blocks
- G-clamps
- chisels
- spring clip
- fine-grade sandpaper
- utility knife

◁ **1** Cut four 4cm/1½in blocks of Cuban mahogany. Saw through the bottom of each of the existing feet to produce flat, square surfaces. Apply glue to the bottom of each foot, then, in the case of the front legs, clamp each block in place with a sash clamp.

2 When clamping the back legs, you will need to compensate for their angle by adding clamping blocks to the sides of each leg with G-clamps. These will provide a purchase for the sash clamps that hold the new wood in place.

◁ **3** When the glue has dried, remove the clamps and start work on one foot by shaping the block with chisels so that it follow the lines of the original foot. Mark the indents carved on the original foot with a pencil.

▷

Extending the feet...continued

◁ **5** Cut small pieces of matching Cuban mahogany to size. Apply PVA (white) glue to the new wood and the existing foot, and press the new wood down firmly.

4 Cut any damaged areas of moulding on the foot flat and parallel with a chisel so that new wood can be glued on and later carved.

6 The replacement moulding covers a very small area, which means that a G-clamp is not suitable. The best method of holding this wood in place while the glue dries is to use a spring clip.

7 When the glue has dried, remove the spring clip. Shape the moulding to match the undamaged areas on the other feet with a bevel-edged chisel.

▷ **8** Finish off the shaping with fine-grade sandpaper. Repeat this process for the mouldings on the other feet.

◁ **10** Cut along the V-shapes in the foot with a tenon saw. Do not cut too deeply – about 1cm/⅜in should be enough.

9 Score along the pencil lines on the foot with a utility knife. This will act as a guide when sawing out the indentations.

11 Begin paring out the V-shape with a narrow chisel. Take care to follow the shape accurately, because any mistakes you make at this stage cannot be corrected.

12 Continue to pare out the V-shape until it matches the depth in the old foot. Try to achieve as smooth a finish as possible.

◁ **13** The restored feet should closely resemble the original ones. The shape of the new feet was determined by researching the various styles of the period in reference books. The feet will be stained and polished once the repairs on the legs have been completed.

Repairing the legs

The legs are worn, and in some areas the carving has been lost completely. Because carved detail can be quite delicate on furniture, it is vulnerable to knocks and scrapes. Over the years, little bits can be broken off. The solution is to glue on new blocks of wood and carve them to shape to reproduce the missing detail. The new wood then needs to be stained and polished to blend it into the original wood. The important requirement is to have some form of reference so that the carvings can be reproduced. Fortunately, in this case it was possible to copy the detail from one leg to another.

MATERIALS AND EQUIPMENT

- chisel
- tenon saw
- Cuban mahogany
- PVA (white) glue
- carving tools
- fine brushes
- bichromate of potash
- polish
- pumice powder
- cloths (cotton rags)
- rubber
- methylated spirits (methyl alcohol)
- wax

1 Trim the groundwork level using a sharp chisel. Cut a piece of straight-grained Cuban mahogany so that it is slightly bigger than the area to be carved, then glue it in place.

2 Using the surviving carving from one of the other legs as a guide, shape the new mahogany roughly to the correct profile with a chisel.

3 Following the design and, more importantly, the style of carving, recarve the missing parts. The skill of the carver in restoration work lies in being able to mimic the hand of the craftsman who originally carved the decoration.

◁ **4** The natural colour of mahogany is redder than is usually desired, so once the carving is complete, brush the new wood with bichromate of potash. This is a chemical stain that will react with the tannin in the wood to produce a more desirable brown.

5 Apply the first layers of polish in thin coats, using a fine brush. This will ensure that all parts of the carving will be polished.

6 Put some polish on a cloth (cotton rag) and sprinkle some fine pumice powder on it, then use this to work the polish into the grain. This process is called fadding. Repeat until the grain is full.

◁ **7** Charge a rubber with polish for the final coats (see pp.39–40) and blend the new work with the existing surface on the legs. Use a cloth to give the original polish a clean using methylated spirits (methyl alcohol), then polish it to revive the surface. Follow this with a dark wax to finish (see p.41). Repeat this process for any other damaged legs.

▷

Rebuilding the chair

Reassembling the chair frame is a straightforward process, but care must be taken to ensure that it is square.

MATERIALS AND EQUIPMENT
- chisel
- PVA (white) glue
- sash clamps
- clamping blocks
- battens
- gauge sticks
- G-clamps

◁ **1** With the new feet glued on and shaped and the legs repaired, the chair can now be rebuilt. Begin by removing any lumps of old glue from the mortise and tenon joints with a chisel. Take care not to reduce the tenon size, as this will result in sloppy joints.

2 Glue the front legs and seat rail together and secure them with a sash clamp and clamping blocks. Check that the legs are spaced correctly by measuring them at top and bottom.

3 Repeat this process for the back legs, then glue the front and back assemblies to the side seat rails to form the seat frame. When clamping the seat frame together, stand the chair on a flat, level surface. Check that the side seat rails are at the same angle by placing a batten of the same size on each and then sighting across them. Their edges should be parallel if the rail angles are the same.

◁ **4** Check that the seat frame is square by measuring the diagonal dimensions with gauge sticks. You can make these from two lengths of wood with the ends cut to points. Hold the rods together so that the points touch diagonally opposing corners. Then, without allowing the rods to shift in your hand, position them between the other two corners. If both dimensions are the same, the seat frame is square. If any adjustment is needed, loosen the clamps, ease the joint(s) in question slightly, then retighten the clamps and check the diagonals again. Leave to dry.

◁ **5** Now glue together the four pieces of the chair back and secure them with sash clamps and clamping blocks. Check the frame for squareness using the gauge sticks. Leave to dry overnight.

6 Apply a generous amount of glue to the area where the back legs meet the seat back upright. This is a particularly fragile area that is easily damaged if the chair is mistreated.

▷ **7** Clamp the back legs and the seat back together, using a G-clamp and clamping blocks. Leave to dry overnight.

▷

FITTING THE CASTORS

Castors were used on 18th-century furniture as a means to lift the pieces slightly and to give an impression of lightness. Their use for moving furniture was less important. This chair was missing the original castors, so suitable alternatives had to be sourced and fitted.

MATERIALS AND EQUIPMENT
- castors
- drill
- wood drill bits
- chisel
- fine-grade sandpaper
- fine brushes
- stain
- polish

1 Try to find castors from a similar period; otherwise select good reproductions from a furniture restoration parts supplier.

2 Find the centre of the foot and drill a clearance hole for the castor spindle. Put the castor on the foot and draw around it. Make sure that the castor sits exactly in the centre.

3 Bore a hole with a diameter that matches the width of the castor base plate, making it almost as deep as the castor and base plate. The wheel should only just be visible when the castor is fitted.

4 Pare around the edge of the hole with a chisel. Continue until the hole is wide enough to accommodate the wheel.

5 Drill a hole for the castor spindle in the centre of the foot, matching the size as closely as possible.

◁ **6** Finish the recess by smoothing it with fine-grade sandpaper, then screw the castor in place. Repeat this process with the other three feet. Finally, use fine brushes to stain and polish the feet to match the rest of the chair.

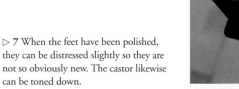

▷ **7** When the feet have been polished, they can be distressed slightly so they are not so obviously new. The castor likewise can be toned down.

FITTING THE BRACKETS

This chair had curved brackets fitted between the seat rails and legs. These were secured originally with glue and dowels. The old dowels have been drilled out and the holes plugged, so the new ones have a secure fixing. The same method of fixing will be employed to refit them, requiring new holes to be drilled in the core wood and new mahogany dowels to be made to match the holes in the brackets.

MATERIALS AND EQUIPMENT
- drill
- wood drill bit
- tenon saw
- mahogany
- hammer
- steel plate
- PVA (white) glue
- chisel
- fine-grade sandpaper

1 Hold the brackets in place and, using a closely matched bit, drill through the dowel holes into the legs and the new core wood or plugged dowel holes of the seat rails.

2 Cut strips of mahogany for the dowels. Hammer them through a hole in a steel plate to round them off and make them the correct diameter.

3 Glue the brackets in place, then knock the dowels through them into the seat rails and legs. Cut down the dowels with a tenon saw, then pare off the remainder with a sharp chisel. Sand them smooth with fine-grade sandpaper.

Right: *Once the chair has been re-upholstered (see pp.67–71) and polished (see pp.39–40), it will look as good as new and should last for another 250 years.*

PROJECT: WINDSOR CHAIR

This 19th-century Windsor chair, made from beech and elm, had been found in a garage. Long forgotten and in a sorry state, it was in need of complete restoration. This required a variety of techniques, since there was a range of damage to be put right. Although such chairs are quite simple in appearance, they are still handsome pieces of furniture and it is worth making an effort to bring them back to their original condition. If the work is done correctly, the result will be a sturdy, good-looking chair that will give many years of service.

ASSESSING THE PROJECT

The most obvious damage is that one arm had broken off. Upon further inspection, it was also discovered that the arm joints in the back upright and shaped seat had broken away and would need replacing. Moreover, the back legs had been reduced in height to give the chair a more reclined feel. This had, however, put an unequal strain on the other legs and stretchers, causing them to become loose. The back legs will therefore need to be removed and returned to their original height. Finally, the seat, unusually for a Windsor chair, had split, and will need to be glued and secured with butterfly keys.

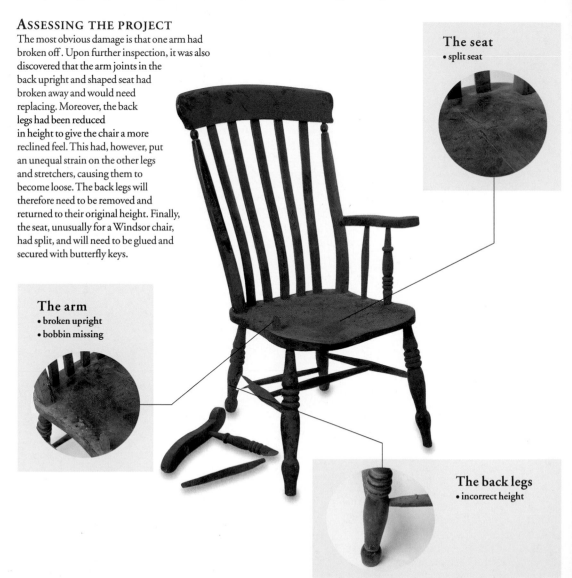

The seat
• split seat

The arm
• broken upright
• bobbin missing

The back legs
• incorrect height

Repairing the seat

The split in the seat had probably been caused by a combination of misuse and climatic changes. Windsor chairs are very robust, and so splits in the seat are relatively uncommon. Fortunately, they are not difficult to repair. The application of glue and butterfly keys will produce a strong seat that will last for many more years to come. There is no need to match the wood of the seat for the butterfly keys; softwood will suffice, and it can be stained to blend in with the original material. You will need a router to cut the recesses for the keys, and, since the chair has a slightly curved surface, a routing guide to provide the router with an even surface to work on.

MATERIALS AND EQUIPMENT	
• tenon saw	• plywood
• softwood	• hammer
• router	• nails
• PVA (white) glue	• plane
• sash clamps	• water-based stain
• clamping blocks	• brush

1 Cut four butterfly keys from a piece of softwood. Remove all the legs, which, due to their condition, should involve no more than simply easing them out. Turn the seat over. Set the stop depth on a router to slightly less than the thickness of the keys.

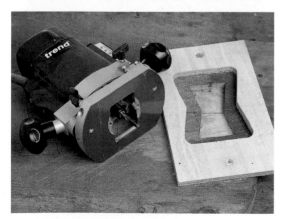

2 Glue the crack, then clamp the seat together using sash clamps and clamping blocks. Cut a plywood routing guide slightly larger than the butterfly keys. Nail this to the underside of the seat where the first key is to be inserted (the waist of each key sits on the crack).

3 Cut the remaining three recesses then glue all the butterflies into position. The crack is now secured.

▷

Repairing the seat...continued

4 Allow the glue to dry. Plane the butterfly keys until they are level with the seat base, then remove the clamps.

◁ **5** Mix a water-based stain to match the wood colour then brush it over the keys. Once the top of the seat has been cleaned and waxed, the crack will be all but invisible.

Repairing the arm

The arm support had broken off at its base. It could not simply be reglued, as the joint would not be strong enough to hold it. A new section would therefore have to be made and fitted.

The bobbin linking the arm to the chair back had been broken off and lost, so a replacement would need to be turned on a lathe.

REPAIRING THE SUPPORT

The arm support was cylindrical in shape and tapered to a narrow point that fitted into a hole in the seat. This shape could not be turned on the lathe, but had to be formed by hand.

MATERIALS AND EQUIPMENT
- drill
- wood drill bit
- beech
- tenon saw
- plane
- paring chisel
- PVA (white) glue
- snap clamp
- spokeshave
- fine-grade sandpaper
- hammer

◁ **1** Remove the broken part of the upright that still remains in the seat by drilling it out from the underside. Choose a drill bit that matches the diameter of the existing hole.

2 Plane the support at an angle and draw a corresponding line on a piece of beech that is slightly bigger than the support.

3 Cut the beech along the line. Plane the end of the longer piece of beech until it is smooth and fits snugly against the support.

4 Glue the support to the centre of the planed end of the beech, and clamp it in position. Leave to dry then remove the clamp.

5 Place the support in a vice and roughly shape the beech with a spokeshave. Continue until it is cylindrical and tapers to a size that will fit in the hole in the seat.

◁ **7** Fit the upright in the chair seat. Check its height against the upright on the other side. If necessary, continue sanding until the correct height has been reached.

6 Smooth the support with sandpaper. Continue until it matches the support on the other arm of the chair, comparing the two often so that you do not remove too much material.

▷

Repairing the support...continued

8 With the suppot inserted in the seat, saw off the excess wood so that it protrudes slightly from the seat.

9 Place the arm support in a vice and use a saw to remove a narrow wedge, about 2.5cm/1in deep, from the bottom of the support.

▷**10** Fit the support back into the seat and apply glue to the wedge-shaped slot. Cut a beech wedge that is marginally larger than the wedge cut out of the support, and hammer it into the slot. This will expand the end of the support, giving a tight joint. When the glue is dry, make the support flush with the underside of the seat using a plane or a paring chisel.

TURNING A BOBBIN

To replace the missing arm bobbin, a new bobbin, with the same dimensions as the bobbin on the undamaged arm, must be turned. This requires skilful lathe work.

MATERIALS AND EQUIPMENT
- drill
- wood drill bits
- beech
- lathe
- turning tools
- dividers
- callipers
- very fine-grade sandpaper
- bench hook
- tenon saw
- PVA (white) glue
- sash clamps
- clamping blocks

◁ **1** Drill out the remainder of the spigot that joined the original bobbin to the back upright. Use a drill bit that corresponds to the diameter of the original hole.

2 Turn a piece of beech to the approximate diameter of the bobbin on the other arm. It is always best to be cautious at this stage; if you over-turn the wood, you will have to start again.

3 Use a pair of dividers, set to the width of the existing bobbin, to mark the new bobbin's position on the rough-turned beech.

4 Use a paring chisel to cut into the wood on each side of the bobbin outline, in preparation for forming the spigots.

5 Continue turning the spigots until they approach the correct diameter, making frequent checks with callipers set to the size of the spigots on the existing bobbin.

◁ **6** Check that the diameter of the spigots is slightly larger than the spigot hole on the arm. This will ensure a good fit and make the joints stronger. Take care, though, that the larger size does not change the balance or proportions of the original piece.

7 Use an angled chisel to turn the bobbin to the correct shape. There is no easy way to do this except with patience and experience. If a mistake is made, the whole process has to be started again. ▷

Turning a bobbin...continued

8 Having turned the bobbin, cut a series of shallow grooves into the two spigots with a turning chisel to give any excess glue somewhere to escape to when the joint is glued. (A joint with too much glue in, and no space for it to escape to, will split the surrounding wood.)

9 With correctly sharpened tools and the proper technique, there should be very little need for much cleaning up, but a final sanding with very fine-grade sandpaper will finish off the turned bobbin. Do not sand the two spigots.

10 Remove the length of beech from the lathe, hold it firmly on a bench hook and cut away the ends with a tenon saw. Make sure you leave enough spigot material to ensure a snug fit in both the back upright and the arm.

11 Use a drill to clean out the spigot hole in the arm. Use a drill bit that corresponds to the size of the new spigot.

12 Glue one spigot into the arm and the other into the back upright. The arm can now be glued to the new support and clamped until dry.

Repairing the legs

The back feet had been reduced in height, making the legs too short, so it is necessary to build them up to make the chair level again. They had been cut off at an angle, so it is not possible simply to glue on extra pieces without them being obvious. The best solution is to replace the whole foot section with a longer version, joining at the old ankle, so that the joint is cleverly disguised. The front original feet can act as a guide to both style and size.

MATERIALS AND EQUIPMENT

- beech
- tenon saw
- steel rule
- drill
- wood drill bits
- lathe
- turning tools
- callipers
- fine-grade sandpaper
- bench hook
- centre finder
- PVA (white) glue
- sash clamps
- fine brush
- spirit-based (alcohol-based) stain
- rubber
- polish
- cloth (cotton rag)
- wax

◁ **1** Select a piece of beech to match the rest of the leg, and cut it to a suitable length and a width larger than the diameter of the foot. Mark the centre of the block on each end with a steel rule and drill a hole about 1cm/⅜in deep at each end.

▷ **2** Cut a shallow groove along a cross-mark at one end with a tenon saw. This drilled and grooved end will house the head stock of the lathe and the end with just the hole will house the tail stock. Both stocks are used to rotate the wood. Measure the existing foot with callipers.

3 Mount the beech in the lathe, then, using a large gouge, roughly turn the wood to the diameter of the widest part of the foot. Do not push the gouge too hard or at too acute an angle, as this could cause it to be "snatched" by the square edges of the wooden block.

4 Use the callipers to mark out the end of the foot and a turning chisel to cut a shallow groove. Then turn a spigot, which will be inserted into the leg.

▷

Repairing the legs...continued

5 Mark a line from which the bulbous shape will be turned, then shape the foot using a skew chisel. Place the bevel against the wood and, after it has been raised and begun to cut, turn it with a smooth rolling action. This will give the required shape.

6 Finish off the shaped foot by gently applying fine-grade sandpaper to remove any tool marks. Cut the excess from the bottom and cut the spigot to the correct length.

7 Place the leg on a bench hook and cut off the shortened foot flush at the ankle. This will mean that the new foot will be attached at a natural joint line, disguising the fact that it is a later replacement.

8 Mark the centre of the leg using a centre finder. This is a useful tool that will enable you to determine the centre of any round item.

9 Drill out the centre of the leg to a diameter that matches the spigot at the top of the new foot. Make sure that the drill is held in line with the leg; it can be helpful to have someone watch you to make sure that the drill does not wander off line.

10 Glue the foot to the leg and use a sash clamp to apply pressure. By attaching the foot in this way, the strength of the joint will be as good as if the leg and foot had been turned from the same piece of wood. Leave to dry, then remove the clamp.

11 Make and attach another foot in the same way, then clean out all the leg and stretcher holes before gluing the joints and reassembling the chair legs and stretchers.

12 Mix a spirit-based (alcohol-based) stain to match the original wood (see p.30), then brush this over the two new feet.

13 Finally, charge a rubber with polish and apply a layer over both new feet (see pp.39–40). Then wax the entire chair so that the repairs blend in (see p.41).

Left: *The restored chair is as good as new and will now sit at the angle originally intended by the maker. The chair will require no further maintenance other than the occasional waxing.*

GLOSSARY

animal glue Also known as scotch glue and traditionally used from the 17th century onwards.

blooming The name given to the white marks left on a polished surface that has been water-damaged or chilled.

bracket foot A square foot which might have a shaped profile on the inside. The foot most commonly used during the 18th century.

breaker A piece or a collection of pieces of furniture used in the restoration of another item of furniture.

bun feet A ball type of foot favoured during the 17th century and replaced by the bracket foot in the 18th century.

butterfly key A butterfly-shaped piece of wood used to secure and hold splits. It is inset into a piece so that the grain runs at right angles to the main wood. Also known as a dovetail key.

carcass The framework of a piece of furniture. Depending on the period, this would be either in the solid or veneered.

cascamite A glue used when forming laminates or shape work. It is very strong but also brittle.

colour The tone or shade that wood develops over time.

conservation To maintain a piece by undertaking as little work as possible so as not to alter its present or original form (*see* restoration).

core The moulded shape on to which veneer or mouldings are applied.

cross-grain mouldings Wood applied to a softwood backing and planed to a moulded profile, applied to a carcass for aesthetic reasons. Introduced during the 17th century, they are more decorative than long-grain mouldings.

Cuban mahogany Mahogany imported from Cuba during the 18th and 19th centuries and the preferred wood for quality furniture. It is densely grained and red in tone when first polished.

de-nibbing The removal of dust that has combined with polish to form small raised nibs on a surface after polishing. This is done by lightly using fine wire wool in the direction of the grain. The surface is then waxed.

dovetail saw A fine-bladed saw used for cutting accurate and delicate dovetails.

fading/fad Filling the grain in wood with a mixture of polish and pumice powder. The cloth with which it is applied is known as a fad.

French curve A kidney-shaped scraper used on concave curves.

French polishing Using shellac polish, which is usually applied with a linen and wadding (batting) rubber.

gauge sticks Two lengths of stick which are held together and used to check the equal diagonal measure of a frame to ensure it is square.

graining Using surface stains and colours to mimic the grain of a solid piece of wood. Favoured during the early 19th century.

Honduras mahogany Mahogany imported from Honduras during the 18th and 19th centuries and favoured for carcass construction.

long-grain mouldings Mouldings planed from one length of wood along the grain and applied to a carcass for aesthetic or structural reasons.

marquetry Inlays of decorative scenes.

mortise The hollow housing part of a mortise and tenon joint, which is the most widely used joint in furniture construction.

mortise gauge A marking tool that has a small steel point and is used along the grain to mark the shoulders of a mortise.

overloe A shaped block used in conjunction with sandpaper.

patera A round or oval, raised decoration often found on cornices or the tops of legs. Can also be used in veneer form.

patination This refers to the build up of waxes, natural greases and dust that over numerous years combines to form a desirable finish on a surface.

PVA glue Polyvinylacetate glue, also known as white glue. Ideal for daily use.

reeded decoration A raised decoration of parallel, tapering lines, usually found on chair and table legs.

reeds Raised dome-shaped decoration applied along the length of a surface.

restoration To undertaken any necessary work to return a piece as near as possible to its original form but retaining its integrity (*see* conservation).

revive a surface The action of attending to any minor damage or surface oxidation of a polished surface while not repolishing the whole top.

rubber Wadding (batting) wrapped in linen, which is used to apply shellac polish.

scratch box A workshop-made tool that allows parallel reeds to be scratched on a leg (*see* reeded decoration).

shellac Polish that is obtained from the shellac beetle.

splay feet A shaped bracket foot that is splayed in profile. Favoured during the late 18th century.

spring clip A workshop-made cramping device made from upholstery springs. Ideal for securing awkward shapes.

stains Usually bought in powder form and mixed with water, spirit or oil depending on the intended use.

tenon The protruding part of a mortise and tenon joint, which is the most widely used joint in furniture construction.

twist When wood bows in two directions.

warp When a piece of wood has bowed along its length or width.

FURTHER INFORMATION

British Antique Furniture Restorers'
Association (BAFRA)
The Old Rectory
Warmwell, Dorchester
Dorset DT2 8HQ
UK
Tel/fax: 01305 854822
Email: headoffice@bafra.org.uk
Web: www.bafra.org.uk

British Antique Dealers'
Association (BADA)
20 Rutland Gate
London SW7 1BD
UK
Tel: 020 7589 4128
Fax: 020 7581 9083
Web: www.bada.org

Association of Art and Antique
Dealers' (LAPADA)
535 Kings Road
Chelsea
London SW10 0SZ
UK
Tel: 020 7823 3511
Fax: 020 7823 3522
Web: www.lapada.co.uk

Association of Restorers
8 Medford Place
New Hartford
NY 13413
USA
Tel: (315) 733–1952
Fax: (315) 724–7231
Web: www.assoc-restorers.com

Art and Antique Dealers' League of
America, Inc. (AADLA)
1040 Madison Avenue
New York
NY 10021
USA
Tel: (212) 879–7558
Fax: (212) 772–7197
www.artantiquedealersleague.com

The National Antique & Art
Dealers Association of America, Inc.
220 East 57th Street
New York
NY 10022
USA
Tel: (212) 826–9707
Fax: (212) 832–9493

Australian Antique Dealers'
Association
PO Box 24
Malvern
Victoria 3144
Australia
Tel: (03) 9576 2275
Fax: (03) 9576 2106
Email: secaada@ozemail.com.au

PICTURE CREDITS

All images © Anness Publishing
Limited, except for: pages 8, 9 t,
10 t b, © Christie's Images.

W.J. COOK & SONS

W.J.Cook & Sons was established by Bill Cook in 1962. His reputation for outstanding work quickly spread and since those early days clients have included the British Royal Household and Government, museums, leading collectors, dealers and private individuals.

While still retaining a London workshop, the business is based in Marlborough, Wiltshire. With the cabinet-making, machine and polishing shops it is a business that is recognized as one of the leaders in its field. After training at the London College of Furniture, three of Bill's sons joined the business and have helped develop and further expand its range and facilities. Now their own children are being encouraged to pick up the tools with a view to taking the family tradition to a third generation.

The services carried out are many and include cabinet-making, gilding, carving, polishing, lock repairs, leathering and upholstery. Being a true family business, every commission is undertaken with great care. With over 40 years of experience at the highest level, together with an extensive in-house library and access to furniture archives, any restoration carried out is authentic in every detail.

Virtually all the restoration work is still carried out using 18th- and 19th-century tools: their band saw was used in the construction of the panelling for the *Queen Mary*.

A final note: antique furniture if badly restored can rarely be returned to its original glory. Therefore, it is important that a suitably qualified restorer should be consulted when necessary.

High Trees House
Savernake Forest
Marlborough
Wiltshire
SN8 4NE
01672 513017

167 Battersea High Street
London
SW11 3JS
020 7736 5329
william.cook@virgin.net
www.wjcookandsons.com

AUTHOR'S ACKNOWLEDGEMENTS

When approached to write this book we were delighted to accept. For a number of years we have been acutely aware of the absence of any book that was written and extensively photographed in a commercial restoration workshop and which showed and explained clearly how various techniques are carried out on a day to day basis. Drawing from over 40 years of experience and a lifetime's collection of materials and tools, we hope that we have given the reader an authoritative insight into the subject.

While the overwhelming majority of work was undertaken "in house", there are grateful thanks due to others who have been invaluable in their help both with advice and in the use of their facilities: Barry Ansell of R.D. Robins Ltd, London, on

upholstery; Geoff Collier of Colliers Castings, Hooe, on casting methods; Les Crispin of Capital Crispin Veneer, London, on veneers, Alan Dallison on leathers, Bob Dunn of A. Dunn & Son, Chelmsford, on marquetry; and Optimum Brasses, Tiverton, on brassware. Thank you.

Special thanks go to the staff in our workshops for making sure that the work needed for this book was always ready on time. A big thank you goes to Paul Lyon for his sterling work, without which this book would have been impossible.

On a personal note, like all family businesses, an unsung hero is our mother Catherine who has always been there keeping the wheels turning. Thanks also to my brothers Richard and Stephen with whom it is very much a team effort, and not to

forget Justin, who has chosen to follow his own path. Thanks to all those who have been encouraging and supportive throughout the whole process of writing this book, including Richard my life-long friend, for his humour, often dispensed from across the world, Nathalie, whose words of wisdom, while not always fully appreciated are always carefully considered, and my three sons William, Henry and James, for just being themselves.

Finally this book is for my father from his sons, and for our sons and daughters from their fathers in the hope that they may one day take the business onwards for another generation.

BILLY COOK

INDEX